BITTER SCENT

BITTER SCENT

The Case of L'Oréal, Nazis, and the Arab Boycott

MICHAEL BAR-ZOHAR

A DUTTON BOOK

DUTTON
Published by the Penguin Group
Penguin Books USA Inc., 375 Hudson Street, New York, New York 10014, U.S.A.
Penguin Books Ltd, 27 Wrights Lane, London W8 5TZ, England
Penguin Books Australia Ltd, Ringwood, Victoria, Australia
Penguin Books Canada Ltd, 10 Alcorn Avenue,
Toronto, Ontario, Canada M4V 3B2
Penguin Books (N.Z.) Ltd, 182–190 Wairau Road, Auckland 10, New Zealand

Penguin Books Ltd, Registered Offices: Harmondsworth, Middlesex, England

First published by Dutton, an imprint of Dutton Signet,
a division of Penguin Books USA Inc.
Distributed in Canada by McClelland & Stewart Inc.

First Printing, November, 1996
10 9 8 7 6 5 4 3 2 1

 REGISTERED TRADEMARK—MARCA REGISTRADA

LIBRARY OF CONGRESS CATALOGING-IN-PUBLICATION DATA
Bar-Zohar, Michael.
    Bitter scent : the case of L'Oréal, Nazis, and the Arab Boycott /
Michael Bar-Zohar.
      p.   cm.
    ISBN 0-525-94068-5
    1. France—Politics and government—1981–   2. Mitterrand,
François, 1916–   —Influence.   3. Frydman, Jean—Relations with
associates.   4. L'Oréal (Firm)—Corrupt practices.   5. Antisemitism—
France.   6. National socialists—France.   7. Jewish-Arab
relations—1973–   I. Title.
DC423.B39   1996
944.083—dc20   96-20383
                                                                   CIP

Printed in the United States of America
Set in Times New Roman
Designed by Jesse Cohen

This book is printed on acid-free paper. ∞

Three friends took the road together.
They went to school in the great city of Paris.
They shared their hopes, their dreams, and their
secrets.
When the war came, they met a rich, strange man.
One of them managed the rich man's business and
made it into an empire.
The second married the rich man's daughter and
became the wealthiest man in the land.
The third won the rich man's support and became
King of France.

1

April 4, 1989, was a cold, rainy day, with sudden gusts of wind swirling through the Centre Eugène Schueller in Paris's drab northern suburb of Clichy. The Centre, a compound of sleek, tall buildings painted in a purple so deep it is almost black, juts up incongruously among run-down, peeling houses, its glass and concrete buildings a darkly foreign presence protected by closed-circuit cameras, floodlights, and uniformed guards.

The severe exterior contrasts sharply with the nature of the product conceived, researched, packaged, and marketed by the thousands of employees working for the Clichy company. Their product is beauty, women's beauty in all its forms. Their creams and oils, lotions and moisturizers, shampoos, conditioners, nail polish, lipsticks, and perfumes are sold worldwide, publicized by luscious models in newspaper ads, billboards, magazine spreads, television commercials, and showcases around the globe. Centre Eugène Schueller is the headquarters of L'Oréal, the world's largest cosmetics company.

In the elegant boardroom on the sixth floor of the main building, the executives of Paravision, a L'Oréal subsidiary, were meeting that morning. Paravision, a firm distributing movies mostly to European television networks, had been created the year before by Jean Frydman, a media wizard, and François Dalle, L'Oréal's aging ex-president. Today's discussion would center on Frydman's proposal to buy the Hollywood giant Columbia Pictures.

Paravision Vice President Jean Frydman was a bald, burly man in his early sixties, with clear blue eyes and a deeply tanned face. Born in Poland, he had come to France at the age of five and lived in Paris most of his life. During World War II he had been a member of the Resistance—the French underground that fought against the Nazi occupation. Though just a teenager, he had distinguished himself by his courage and dedication, blowing up German trains, power lines, and strategic plants, and participating in many bloody battles against German soldiers. Captured by the Gestapo and sentenced to death, Frydman survived only by a miracle. When the war ended, he was decorated as a hero. The young man embarked from there on a brilliant career in the media and became a leading radio and television executive. Although he was staunchly French, and had many friends in high places, after the Six-Day War in 1967 he felt a growing bond with Israel. Finally, in 1981, he moved there with his young wife, built a house in a Tel Aviv suburb, and applied for Israeli citizenship.

Also at the board meeting was bearlike François Dalle, a bald man with heavy-rimmed glasses set atop a bulbous nose. Dalle had known Jean Frydman since the late fifties, when Frydman had become one of the managers of Europe 1, a radio station that carried a considerable portion of L'Oréal's advertising. As recently as the year before, in 1988, Dalle had been invited to spend the Christmas vacation in Frydman's house in Israel, where Frydman had introduced him to Shimon Peres, Ariel Sharon, and other Israeli leaders.

After retiring from L'Oréal's presidency in 1984, Dalle had remained on the board as an adviser to his successors. That same year he was appointed president of the strategic committee of L'Oréal, a new group created to define basic corporate goals. He also was vice president of Nestlé, the huge Swiss-based conglomerate specializing in milk products, which owned a large block of L'Oréal shares.

L'Oréal's employees used to joke that Paravision was François Dalle's *danseuse*, or chorus girl, a secret passion to which the seventy-one-year-old man had finally succumbed after many years devoted to making L'Oréal a business empire. The old man now dreamed of the glamorous life of a movie producer, they said, and wanted to spend his last years in the company of film producers, directors, and stars. They also hinted that the new president of L'Oréal, a forty-year-old Welshman by the name of Lindsay Owen-Jones, was more than happy to let his illustrious predecessor play the Hollywood mogul, even if it cost L'Oréal a few million dollars. That left "O.J."— as the employees called Owen-Jones—to run L'Oréal as he wished.

Paravision was structured like L'Oréal, its board of directors a mere rubber stamp for the decisions of its own strategic committee, chaired by Paravision's president, Michel Pietrini. A slim man whose youthful face was dominated by deep, vulnerable black eyes, he was a former executive of Chanel perfumes. Among the other members of the strategic committee was Jean-Pierre Meyers, the son-in-law of L'Oréal's principal stockholder, André Bettencourt.

That morning in April 1989, Jean Frydman was dressed in a conservative dark gray suit as he stood by a blackboard and explained the details of his ambitious proposal to buy Columbia Pictures.

The Coca-Cola Company, he said, was ready to sell its controlling stock in Columbia for $2 billion, and Frydman had worked out a tentative deal with the Westinghouse Company for a fifty-fifty partnership in the buyout of Columbia. Westinghouse would get the California studios while Paravision obtained the extensive film library, thus becoming the world's largest movie owner and distributor. "This will be the achievement of my lifelong dream," he concluded.

At this point François Dalle spoke up.

Frydman expected only support from his colleague. A few days before, he had run into Dalle on a street corner in Marbella, where the Frydmans were vacationing. It turned out the Dalles were also spending a few days at the Mediterranean coastal resort. Dalle, returning from a game of golf, asked the Frydmans to have dinner with him and his wife. Afterward, Dalle and Frydman had parted on the best of terms. But now Dalle seemed to have reservations about the Columbia deal.

"This buyout involves a huge investment," he said. "I think Nestlé should be involved in the operation."

The Nestlé company owned 49 percent of Gesparal, the holding company controlling 51 percent of L'Oréal's stock. L'Oréal owner André Bettencourt, the richest man in France—and probably the second richest in Europe after Queen Elizabeth—owned 51 percent of Gesparal. His fortune came from his marriage to Liliane Schueller, the daughter of L'Oréal's founder.

Frydman turned to the other members of the strategic

committee. "We are trying to borrow most of the necessary funds from the Crédit Suisse," he told them, naming one of the big-three Swiss banks. "In a few days," he added, "François Dalle and I shall be going to Geneva to meet the Crédit Suisse president, Mr. Gutt, and negotiate the loan."

The next to intervene was Marc Ladreit de Lacharrière, L'Oréal's vice president and top financial expert. Lacharrière, a younger man, was not a member of Paravision's strategic committee, but had been invited to the meeting because a move of great financial import was being discussed. "I'd like to ask you a few questions, Jean," he said pleasantly. "If we conclude a deal with the Crédit Suisse they'll want to be informed about Paravision's assets. Could you give us some details about your part of the shares?"

Jean Frydman and his younger brother, David, had invested $50 million, financed by the sale to Paravision of their library of about 1,800 American, French, and Italian films whose European rights the Frydmans had owned since the mid-fifties. L'Oréal had invested the other three-quarters, or $150 million, in the company.

"Ten percent of the shares belong to a French company owned by my family," Frydman answered. The remaining fifteen percent, he said, were held by a Dutch company and some Israeli companies he owned. In Israel he was represented by Michael Feron, an Israeli lawyer.

"Ah, Israel," said François Dalle, clearly ill at ease. "There is this problem of the Arab boycott, and I don't want to embarrass Owen-Jones." He turned to Lacharrière. "Why don't you explain to Jean what the problem is."

"What problem?" Frydman asked, surprised. He had

come to report to the strategic committee about his Columbia project. Instead, they were suddenly talking about
the Arab boycott.

Dalle then reviewed L'Oréal's acquisition a few years
ago of Helena Rubinstein, a major American cosmetics
company with scores of affiliates throughout the world.
The deal had been negotiated by Cosmair, L'Oréal's
American affiliate. But Helena Rubinstein figured on the
blacklist of the Arab Boycott Bureau, a boycott effort
aimed against Israel, because the late Ms. Rubinstein, a
prominent American Zionist, had built a plant in Israel.

Frydman was familiar with the activities of the Boycott Bureau, which had been created by the Arab League
after the birth of the State of Israel. Its purpose was to
ban all trade and business dealings with any company that
established economic ties with Israel. Such a company
couldn't sell its products in any Arab country until it
proved that it had cut all its relations with Israel. The goal
of the boycott was to strangle Israel's economy, and it had
met with considerable success. Israel estimated the boycott damage at about $20 billion in exports and $16 billion
in investments over a period of forty-five years.

The boycott was considered illegal by most Western
governments, and many countries, including France, had
adopted tough antiboycott laws that explicitly prohibited
complying with the bureau's boycott demands or even
answering its questionnaires. But legislation was one
thing, and business another. Following the acquisition
of Helena Rubinstein by L'Oréal, the Arab League had
extended the boycott and blacklisted L'Oréal as well.
Now, as a preliminary condition to lifting the boycott, the
Boycott Bureau had sent a questionnaire to L'Oréal and
demanded answers.

The Paravision strategic committee meeting took a

turn for the worse. Jean Frydman stared at François Dalle in disbelief while Marc Ladreit de Lacharrière started firing his questions: Did L'Oréal manufacture any cosmetics in Israel? How did Frydman stand in regard to L'Oréal in Israel? What were Frydman's connections in Israel and what was the nature of his affairs there?

Although Frydman knew that complying with Arab boycott demands was strictly illegal, he tried to contain his anger, mostly because of his friendship with François Dalle.

"Frydman was shocked by these questions," a participant in the meeting later testified, "because according to his own words, Israel's well-being was his major goal. This questioning, in the presence of everybody, was hard; usually one doesn't discuss these kinds of matters in public."

Frydman told Lacharrière that, while his affairs in Israel were nobody's business, he would answer the questions nevertheless. He held dual French and Israeli citizenship, and since the early eighties he had been a resident of Israel. He owned a company there that managed the advertising on the national radio. Another venture of his was the construction of the Israeli telecommunications satellite Amos.

The mention of the satellite seemed to worry both Dalle and Lacharrière. They asked if it was a purely Israeli project. Somebody mentioned that it might have military uses as well.

"My partners in that endeavor," Frydman said, "are General Hod, the former chief of the Israeli Air Force, and General Amit, former chief of the Mossad."* Then

* The Mossad is the Israeli intelligence agency, roughly similar to the American CIA.

he added sarcastically: "You can tell this to your friends at the Boycott Bureau."

Frydman's words shook his audience. After a moment of tense silence, François Dalle turned to Frydman again and said, "The Arab League demands that we provide them with a list of all our affiliates, and the names of the members of our board, before they decide to lift the boycott. This is very important for L'Oréal, but even more for Nestlé." Since the Arab markets accounted for at least 15 percent of Nestlé's global exports of milk products, an extension of the boycott to Nestlé could be disastrous. Dalle continued, "I am talking to you in my capacity as vice president of Nestlé as well. Would you be willing to resign from your Israeli activities?"

"You must be joking," Frydman said. He was outwardly calm, but his fists were clenched. How can he ask such a thing of me? he thought. Does he think I am that sort of man? Just then he fleetingly recalled a scene from the early days of the Nazi occupation of France, when a French friend of his father had crossed the street to avoid being seen with a Jew.

Dalle pointed out that Frydman could resign temporarily from Paravision until the boycott problem was solved, then retake his seat in a year's time. He was joined by another L'Oréal executive who told Frydman that he should change his address, because his Israeli residence might expose L'Oréal to the Arab boycott. A member of Paravision's board, Michael Stevens, who also participated in the meeting, later said, "It was clear . . . that if Frydman wanted to maintain his partnership with L'Oréal, he either had to change his country of residence, or resign in favor of a representative of his choice who had an acceptable address."

Frydman firmly refused. He added, though, that the following year he intended to become a French resident

again because he wanted his young daughter to go to
school in France. Therefore L'Oréal's problem would
cease to exist.

That didn't satisfy François Dalle. "Perhaps you
would like to appoint somebody to replace you on the
board until you come back?" he insisted.

"No," Frydman said and concluded, "I don't want to
embarrass you, but I shall never resign, and I hope that
this is clear."

The meeting ended. Frydman went home, humiliated
and insulted. "They thought I would accept their disgusting offer," he told his wife, Daniela, that night. "Is that
what they think of me?" He had been so proud to embark
upon a joint venture with a highly respectable French
company, and this was how they were treating him. He
thought that in these conditions his partnership with
L'Oréal in Paravision might not last. But he had invested
all his property in Paravision, and he had brought over his
brother and all his team. He couldn't give up now. He
decided to stay on and hope that nothing changed.

At first nothing did. Three days after the meeting,
Frydman went to Geneva with Dalle to discuss the Crédit
Suisse loan for the acquisition of Columbia. The two men
enjoyed each other's company as usual, and the trip was
a success, although the Columbia deal later fell through.
The company was finally acquired by Sony for a much
higher price. Frydman then returned to his Paravision office on the Champs-Élysées. The question of the boycott
wasn't mentioned anymore. Frydman believed the affair
was closed.

He was wrong. The war was just beginning.

The name L'Oréal is a combination of the old Greek
word *orea*, meaning "beauty," and the Latin *aureola*, or

"golden crown." With an annual gross of $7 billion, the conglomerate employs 30,000 people in France alone and thousands of other people in more than 140 countries. Besides its own products, it owns the famous cosmetics trademarks Lancôme, Helena Rubinstein, Cacharel, Biotherm, Guy Laroche, Ralph Lauren, Giorgio Armani, Paloma Picasso, and Lanvin. It also controls women's magazines, laboratories, pharmaceutical plants, and research institutes. Its American exclusive agent, Cosmair, is the second largest cosmetics company in the U.S., after Revlon. In France, L'Oréal's advertising budget amounts to 40 percent of all the moneys spent on advertising.

Since its creation in 1988, its subsidiary Paravision had established several branches in Europe and acquired a few companies abroad. Its goal was to establish twenty-two subsidiaries in various countries to distribute the movies from its film library, the largest outside the U.S. It had already bought the Dino De Laurentiis company for $60 million and Filmation, the world's third largest cartoon production company, for $30 million. The acquisition of the latter had brought into the library a six-hundred-hour collection of popular cartoons like *He-Man & She-Ra* and *Ghostbusters*. Yet that particular deal had frustrated Jean Frydman, because Michel Pietrini, Paravision's president, had let slip through his fingers a property Frydman considered extremely valuable—the *Teenage Mutant Ninja Turtles* series.

On June 22, 1989, eleven weeks after the April 4 meeting, a young secretary in Paravision's legal department knocked on Jean Frydman's door at Paravision's headquarters. "I am sorry to interrupt," she said, "but we can't find your letter of resignation in our files. I brought another letter for you to sign. It's the standard form."

Frydman stood up, livid. "What letter? I never re-signed!"

"Oh, yes, you did," the young woman said. "Your resignation was approved by the board of directors."

"What board of directors?" Frydman roared. "When was there a board meeting? And what resignation?"

The secretary didn't know what to say.

Frydman was beside himself with anger. That morning he had heard rumors that certain L'Oréal executives were trying to oust him from Paravision U.K., the English branch of his company. In fact, he had summoned Michael Stevens, Paravision U.K.'s president, who had been vigorously denying such a move when the secretary walked in. And now, right in the middle of their conversation, this young woman was calmly asking for his letter of resignation.

"Where's Pietrini?" Frydman shouted. "I want Pietrini here right away!"

A few minutes later Michel Pietrini walked into Frydman's office followed by Catherine Morisse, the head of the legal department. Michael Stevens remained in the room.

Frydman barely controlled himself. "What have you done?" he yelled at Pietrini. "What's this story about my resignation?"

"It was officially approved by a board of directors decision," Pietrini said. "We have the documents."

"What decision? When did the board of directors meet? I was never invited to such a meeting!"

"The date on record is March 30, 1989," Pietrini said. "I thought you had agreed to resign at the strategic committee meeting."

"You must be out of your mind!" Frydman shouted. "I never said I was going to resign!"

Pietrini seemed at a loss. "I knew this was going to end badly," he finally admitted. "This is because of the boycott affair. It is not my fault. It is the doing of Corrèze. He is in charge of the negotiations with the Arabs from the Boycott Bureau."

"Corrèze? Who is Corrèze?"

Pietrini took a deep breath. "You won't like the answer."

"Who is he?"

"Corrèze is the president of L'Oréal's affiliate in New York, Cosmair."

"So?"

"He is a former Nazi," Pietrini said. "After the war he was condemned by a French court to a long prison term for his crimes under Vichy." By this he meant the collaborationist government of Marshal Pétain, which had cooperated with the Germans from 1940 to 1944, and had established its capital in the small southern city of Vichy.

Frydman was stunned. What did an ex-Nazi criminal have to do with his fraudulent resignation?

Catherine Morisse too was stunned—and torn. She owed her position at Paravision to Jean Frydman. A slim blonde, she was the daughter of the late Lucien Morisse, Frydman's former partner at Europe 1. Frydman had always treated Catherine with affection—some said like an adopted daughter—and had brought her with his team to Paravision. Catherine Morisse also was a close friend of Jean Frydman's eldest daughter. But the young Ms. Morisse was chief of the legal department now, loyal above all to her boss, Michel Pietrini.

It was she who had sent her secretary to Jean Frydman to get his resignation letter. Pietrini had informed her, a few months before, that Jean had decided to resign.

She had taken several steps following that conversation. Although she knew there had been no board of directors meeting on March 30, 1989, it was common practice at L'Oréal to hold board meetings only on paper. Top executives would meet informally, make their decisions, then formalize them by instructing their staff to write them up as if they had been made at a board meeting. The practice was illegal, but nobody seemed to care. Pietrini had instructed Catherine Morisse to prepare an official account of a board of directors meeting and date it March 30, 1989. He told her that Jean Frydman's resignation was to be the subject of that fictitious board meeting. Morisse prepared the necessary document and routinely sent it to the Clavier law firm, L'Oréal's legal counsel. The Clavier attorneys, just as routinely, approved and certified the authenticity of the account.

It had never crossed Ms. Morisse's mind to ask Frydman if the information about his departure was true. If not for his missing letter of resignation, he might not have learned for a long while that he had "resigned."

She now hurriedly left the room, unwilling to become caught in the crossfire between her boss and her mentor.

"A former Nazi had me ousted from my company?" Frydman shouted at Pietrini. "You're crazy, all of you!"

He couldn't believe what he had just heard. The president of Cosmair was a former Nazi? What would a Nazi criminal be doing in such a respectable company as L'Oréal? And how had a former Nazi been admitted to the United States?

He stormed out of his room and into his brother's office. Their secretary, Tania Sciama, had never seen her boss so furious. David Frydman listened to him in astonishment. In the space of a few minutes Jean had found that he had been fraudulently dismissed, that L'Oréal had yielded to the Arab boycott, and that one of the L'Oréal bosses, the man responsible for his ouster, was Jacques Corrèze, a convicted Nazi.

David Frydman had admired his older brother since his childhood, when Jean was a freedom fighter. A short man with receding white hair and a square mustache, David was seven years Jean's junior. Their parents had come to France in 1938 from Poland with two children—Jean and his sister. But as foreigners they wouldn't be allowed to stay in France unless they had a child born in French territory. That's why David came into the world in Lens, in the *département* of Pas-de-Calais. He called himself "a child of the Republic."

Unlike Jean, David was not a businessman. He dreamed of changing the world and had fiery antimilitaristic views. Drafted into the French army and sent to Algeria to fight the Arab rebellion, he had refused to use a weapon and had been sentenced to three months in jail. After his return to Paris, he had studied electronic engineering and spent several years as a government employee.

At the end of the seventies, when Jean started planning his move to Israel, he had asked David to enter the business and take his place at the head of the movie distribution company. David had agreed, and had been enthralled by the new world he discovered. He shared his brother's dream of developing Paravision into a major player in the field.

He was stupefied by Jean's account of his meeting with Michel Pietrini.

On Jean's demand, a secretary brought them the minutes of the Paravision board meeting where he allegedly had resigned. According to the document, all the members of the board had been present, including Jean and David Frydman. The only subject on the agenda was "Resignation of Mr. Jean Frydman from his functions as member of the board and vice president."

The minutes ran: "The President reads before his colleagues the resignation letter of Mr. Jean Frydman . . . effective as from April 1, 1989.

"The board accepts that resignation while regretting it and decides that [Mr. Frydman] will not be replaced."

Jean Frydman decided to turn to his friends in high places—to the Élysée, the presidential palace—for help. He knew that President François Mitterrand was personally involved in France's antiboycott policy. In 1981, at the beginning of his first term, Mitterrand had kept his campaign promise and declared illegal any compliance with boycott demands. Prime Minister Pierre Mauroy published a decree canceling an executive order, issued by his predecessor, Raymond Barre, which bypassed the existing legislation and in essence tolerated the boycott. He declared, "Our trade system must not include any discrimination, whatever its reason."

Mitterrand had then set up a secret committee that operated in the Élysée Palace, including among its outstanding members future U.N. ambassador Claude de Kemoularia, Mitterrand's advisers Charles Salzmann and Hubert Védrine, and a famous law professor, Jean-Louis Bismuth, who had been the primary legal mind behind the French antiboycott laws.

The committee was instructed to prepare the new antiboycott strategy. The president's guidelines to the committee stressed that, besides putting an end to all discrimination, the new measures "should preserve France's essential trade with the countries that apply the boycott legislation." Kemoularia had done a superb job in Paris, then discreetly toured the Arab capitals, making clear to the Middle East leaders that from now on France would strictly enforce the antiboycott legislation.

From his brother's office Jean Frydman now called the presidential palace, hoping to obtain the assistance of Mitterrand's staff. He was invited to meet with his friend Charles Salzmann, the president's adviser. A half hour later, Salzmann listened gravely, then said, "Would you like to see our man who is in charge of the boycott?"

They crossed the courtyard of the Palais de l'Élysée and went to the office of Marc Boudier, a young economist and Mitterrand's assistant.

Boudier, as a member of the Élysée antiboycott committee, had traveled with Ambassador de Kemoularia to many Arab capitals. He listened to Frydman's story and said angrily, "The facts you report are extremely serious. What the L'Oréal people are doing is absolutely illegal. They should have refused to deal with the boycott and come to us for help. That is our job!" He added, "If any legal proceedings are undertaken, we will be willing to press charges."

That night Frydman and his wife were having dinner with a close friend, Anne Sinclair, one of France's most popular television show hostesses. Frydman, still upset, described the morning's events and the role of Corrèze.

"I'm not surprised," Sinclair said. "I've heard that quite a few former collaborators found jobs at L'Oréal after the war. Some people at L'Oréal helped one of them, Jean Leguay, to become secretary of the French perfume industry association. My father, who had a perfume shop, resigned in protest."

Jean felt a fresh surge of fury. Corrèze hadn't been the only war criminal to find refuge at L'Oréal. What sort of vipers' nest was he uncovering? Late that night, he started calling experts on the Vichy regime, including the police officer turned historian Jacques Delarue, the famous Nazi hunter Serge Klarsfeld, and the journalist Michele Cotta, who had written a book on Vichy's collaboration with the Nazis. He also spoke, several days later, with the president of the League of Human Rights, Henri Noguères. "Have you heard about a man named Corrèze?" he asked each of them.

The answers varied between astonishment and disbelief. "Corrèze is a bloody criminal," one of his interlocutors said. "But he is long dead!"

"I thought he lived in exile in Spain," somebody offered. "Before the war he was one of the leaders of La Cagoule, the extreme right-wing underground."

"Corrèze?" said another. "I would love to lay my hands on him. But where is he?"

Nobody, however, was able to provide a satisfactory answer about Corrèze's war crimes. Frydman asked his wife to visit the Center of Contemporary Jewish Documentation and look for documents about Corrèze. Daniela returned with a meager but significant harvest: a few documents partly describing Corrèze's activities during the war. One of them mentioned his membership in the notorious Cagoule. Another was a short curriculum vitae written by Corrèze himself in 1942:

Jacques Corrèze . . . born 11 February 1912 in Auxerre . . .

Arrested by the Blum government on 1 July 1938 . . . released from prison 28 August 1939 . . . fought in the 1939–1940 war in a tank unit.

From July 1940 to September 1941, worked at the Mouvement Social Révolutionnaire with Monsieur Deloncle. Joined the Legion of French Volunteers in

Russia in September 1941 . . . was discharged in April 1942.

Even these few lines indicated that Corrèze was a dedicated Nazi. Only the most fanatical pro-German activists had volunteered to fight in Russia.

Frydman's knowledge was augmented when, a few weeks later, he had lunch with his friend Valéry Giscard d'Estaing, France's former president. Since his defeat in the 1981 presidential election, Giscard had spent two of his summers on Frydman's ranch in Canada, riding in cowboy boots, jeans, and checked shirts. He also had been a guest in Frydman's home in Israel and met there with the nation's leaders.

The luncheon took place at the Château de l'Étoile, an ancient castle belonging to Anne-Aymone Giscard d'Estaing, near the city of Angers. The former president had also invited Mr. Jean Sérisé, his former chief of staff. As they sat in the pleasant dining room, decorated with paintings of hunting scenes and big game trophies, tusks, and stuffed lion heads, Jean Frydman described the events surrounding his unseating and mentioned the role of Jacques Corrèze.

Neither Giscard nor Jean Sérisé was surprised by the story. Giscard said that some notorious war criminals had belonged to the secret right-wing organization called La Cagoule—the Cowl. "Eugène Schueller, L'Oréal's founder," he noted, "was one of the Cagoule leaders and its main financial supporter. After the war he brought some of his former friends into L'Oréal."

Following that luncheon, Sérisé sent Frydman a book entitled *Dagore—The Secret Diaries of La Cagoule* by the historian Christian Bernadac. The book exposed the dark terrorist plots and assassinations perpetrated by La Cagoule, and its ambitions to overthrow the French regime by a violent coup d'état. It also described the secret activities of Jacques Corrèze.

There could be no more doubt. L'Oréal's representative in the United States, the secret negotiator with the Arab Boycott Bureau and the mastermind behind Frydman's ouster, was a Nazi criminal. Frydman was deeply shaken.

He also had an odd feeling of déjà vu. During the war the most painful part of his clandestine activities had been fighting fellow Frenchmen who had collaborated with the German occupiers. Most of the French people had passively cooperated with the Germans, and a number had taken part in Nazi war crimes. Thousands of young Frenchmen had volunteered for the German army; thousands of others had joined the pro-German Milice and willingly assisted the Nazis in fighting the Resistance units. The French police had also collaborated with the Nazis and delivered to them scores of thousands of French Jews for deportation to the death camps.

This inglorious chapter in France's recent history left a deep wound on the country's psyche. Many Frenchmen continue to feel ashamed of their countrymen's collaboration with the enemy, and ugly truths about that period keep emerging in political debates, books, and newspaper articles. Several trials of former French collaborators are still under way today in France.

Jean Frydman was haunted by memories from his past as a Resistance member. Still, at the end of the war, he felt that justice had triumphed. For him the years after the defeat of Germany had been a happy period. The Resistance had won, its leaders were in power, and the collaborators with the Nazis had been punished. Frydman had been a witness for the prosecution at the trials of two notorious collaborators, David and Rotte, the chief commissioners of the special "anti-terrorist" brigades. They had been found guilty and shot. The good guys had won and the bad guys had been punished.

Yet now one of those he had believed punished was once more confronting him. Jacques Corrèze had made a brilliant career at L'Oréal, and was now trying to oust Frydman from Paravision because he was Jewish. Forty-five years after the defeat of Nazism, Frydman's vilest enemies were emerging out of the shadows to haunt him again.

2

Jean Frydman was barely fifteen, a curly-haired boy in short pants from the Jewish neighborhood of Belleville, when the German army marched into Paris on that fateful day of June 14, 1940. He stood by the Porte des Lilas fighting his tears as helmeted Wehrmacht soldiers driving motorcycles with sidecars roared down the deserted avenues of the French capital.

France's defeat had been swift and utterly humiliating. On May 10, 1940, eight months after the outbreak of World War II and the collapse of Poland, the German army had attacked France. Hitler's armored divisions had breached the French front and swept through the country encountering almost no resistance. Paris was soon occupied, and two days later a new government, headed by eighty-four-year-old Marshal Philippe Pétain, surrendered to Germany. On June 22, Hitler came to the signing of France's capitulation at Rethondes, at the exact spot where Germany had signed her own capitulation at the end of World War I.

Hitler dismembered France into six zones. The eastern provinces of Alsace-Lorraine were annexed to Germany. The southeast of France was occupied by fascist Italy. Several northeastern regions were attached to Belgium, which had also been occupied by the Germans. A "forbidden" zone was established along the English Channel, designed for military purposes.

The bulk of French territory was divided in two main zones: the "occupied zone" in the north, including Paris, and the "free zone" in the south. For this a puppet French government was established in the small city of Vichy. Its head was Marshal Pétain, a hero of World War I but by this point a docile old man who did what the Germans told him to do. Although it was located in the free zone, the Vichy government was given authority over several services in the occupied zone, including the Paris police.

Pétain proceeded to abolish the French republic and its institutions, adopt anti-Semitic legislation, and solemnly declare that France would collaborate with Nazi Germany. René Bousquet, who was later appointed police secretary-general, put the police force under the Germans' orders. At first, most Frenchmen enthusiastically endorsed Pétain's leadership. One exception was General Charles de Gaulle, who had crossed the Channel, reached London, and appealed to the French people to fight against Germany and liberate their country. He was joined by a handful of patriots who called themselves the Free French.

Jean couldn't believe that his beloved France, the greatest, strongest, most beautiful country in the world, had been so easily defeated by the Nazis. In his eyes, France should never have submitted. Then and there he decided that there was only one way for him and the rest of the French people: to unite and launch an armed rebellion against the Germans.

That fall, on November 11, 1940, he took part in a spontaneous protest against the Nazi occupation that swept the Champs-Élysées. For the first time since the fall of France an angry, defiant crowd shouted, *"Vive de Gaulle! Vive de Gaulle!"* A few people sang the national anthem, "La Marseillaise." The French police, following the orders of their German masters, rounded up hundreds of protesters and beat them.

Skinny young Jean Frydman was arrested too and taken with other prisoners to the Grand Palais, a sprawling building off the Champs-Élysées. The police, though, kept him for only twenty-four hours, wrote down his name, and sent him home. After all, he looked like a child. "Remember, kid," an officer said to him, "next time we meet, you're in trouble."

The next time Jean got caught was a month later, at the Spanish border. In December 1940 he decided to illegally cross the border into neutral Spain, sail to England, and join de Gaulle's Free French forces in London.

In order to reach Spain, however, he had to cross not one but two borders. First was the armistice line between German-occupied France in the north and the Vichy-governed south. This one he negotiated successfully. The teenager stole fifty francs from his mother, took the train to Poitiers, and calmly crossed the line into the free zone in full view of the German soldiers. He already knew that nobody would be suspicious of a kid in short pants.

Jean reached the city of Pau by bus. Pau was nestled at the foot of the Pyrenees Mountains that separated France from Spain. Jean tried to cross the Spanish frontier on Christmas Eve. Unfortunately, he was caught, tried, and sentenced to three months in jail. But once again the police released the brat in short pants after a mere fortnight.

For the following three months Jean lived with a Jewish family, the Bojmals. Before the war Madame Bojmal had been employed in Jean's parents' lingerie workshop. During this period Jean fell in love for the first time. In Pau he met another Jewish refugee from Paris—a blond, blue-eyed girl with a heart-shaped face. Her name was Angela, but he called her *l'Ange*—the Angel. The two youngsters used to walk about the picturesque city holding hands. A couple of times they bashfully kissed.

For a while life seemed idyllic. Pau was far from the cruel realities of the war. But Jean wanted to go back and fight. Finally Madame Bojmal wrote a letter to his mother, and Madame Frydman traveled all the way down from Paris to pick up the young troublemaker. Jean bade farewell to the Angel, though her face would keep haunting him for the rest of the war. Often he dreamed of the day when he would participate in the liberation of France, and then, a hero, he would come to Pau to rescue Angela.

Back in Paris, Jean didn't return to school, fearing the police had been notified of his attempt to cross the Spanish border and would arrest him when he came to class. Besides, he didn't want to go to school anymore; he wanted to fight for liberation. His mother tried to dissuade him. He was her favorite child, and she worried terribly about him. But in June 1941 he ran away from home again and traveled to Nice, on the Mediterranean coast.

A friend in Pau had given him the name and address of a painter in Nice who was supposed to be a member of the Resistance. "I'll take you," the man said, "but first of all you have to get false ID papers."

How did one get a false identity card in wartime France? Jean heard that a camp of the Compagnons de France, the pro-Pétain youth movement, had been built in the hills overlooking Nice. He traveled to the camp and was admitted, using the name René Savary. He spent two months there posing as a gentile, wearing the Compagnons' uniform and singing "Maréchal, nous voilà!"—the anthem glorifying Marshal Pétain. When he finally returned to Nice, he carried in his wallet genuine papers identifying him as René Savary.

He was frustrated with the early missions he carried out for the Resistance—delivering letters and messages. But after a few months he met a man named Michel Bonnerre who told him, "If you want real action, I can introduce you to somebody who is in charge of a commando unit."

In that unit Jean saw action for the first time. His new comrades taught him to use explosives and firearms. Jean participated in several sabotage operations against strategic objectives, like railroads and power lines in the Nice area, and took part in a vain attempt to blow up the Anthéor viaduct connecting France and Italy.

At first the commandos were poorly armed, but British submarines unloaded several crates of weapons and explosives in the bay of Saint-Tropez. Once the small team of freedom fighters was equipped with this material, their operations grew more daring and effective.

In early July 1942, Jean heard from an informer in the local police about the impending arrest of Jews in Paris. He decided to warn his family and tried to sneak into the occupied zone, but was seized by the Germans at a checkpoint. He spent eight days in Tours prison, shining German soldiers' boots. When he was released, he traveled to Paris and convinced his parents to escape with his sister and his little brother, David, into the free zone.

In November 1942 the Allies landed in North Africa. Fearing an invasion of the south of France, the German army immediately occupied the free zone. The Gestapo—

Hitler's secret police—fanned out through the Vichy-controlled areas. The government was left in place, but it became impotent. At the Mediterranean port of Toulon, rather than delivering their navy into the hands of the Germans, the French sailors rigged their ships with explosives and blew them up off France's shores.

The Gestapo and the Milice—a paramilitary organization of fascist French collaborators—now began arresting, torturing, and executing freedom fighters in the south. In addition, the Jews living in the formerly "free" zone were doggedly persecuted by the Germans and their French supporters; many of them were deported to Germany and Poland.

Jean and his friends carried on with their Resistance operations, killing several Gestapo informers among other deeds. But by May 1943 most of the members of Jean's group had been captured.

Jean himself succeeded in escaping to Grenoble and then to the *département* of the Creuse, where his parents were living in the home of a Gentile farmer. The Creuse, a land of hills and forests, occupies the very center of France. The mayor of the village where the Frydman family lived helped Jean get in touch with the local Resistance group, which belonged to the organization FTP (Francs-Tireurs et Partisans) and was named the Estienne d'Orves Commando after the first French patriot to have been executed by the Germans. At this time the group was living in a rudimentary camp in the forest, badly equipped and desperately in need of weapons. Finally, on the night of June 16, 1943, a shipment of arms was parachuted over their field camp by a British plane.

Jean, who had never been good with his hands, learned to take apart and reassemble a submachine gun, blindfolded, with lightning speed. He also became an explosives expert. The youth soon joined a sabotage team that blew up high-voltage power lines, railroad tracks, and German trains. Their goal was to destroy the transport and communications lines the Germans used, anticipating an Allied landing. The team blew up thirteen trains in the next few months. Jean was particularly proud of the night they destroyed a train carrying torpedoes for German U-boats to the Mediterranean port of Sète.

In the summer Jean was sent with a small team to the neighboring *département* of the Indre to blow up trains and a military transmitter used for communications with the German U-boat fleet. The underground fighters were betrayed by a local farmer and attacked by six hundred fascist Milice members. In the violent battle that ensued, five of Jean's friends were killed and another three taken prisoner. Still, they came away with a measure of satisfaction. They left seventeen Milice dead and a large number wounded.

Back in the Creuse, Jean and his comrades continued their sabotage operations. At age eighteen Jean Frydman, now known as Jeannot, became a "team commander." He led a small group of men in regular firefights against the area Milice and attacks on their camps. Growing numbers of German troops and French collaborators started hunting them, even using light aircraft to spot them.

During the bitterly cold fall of 1943, the freedom fighters slept in holes they dug in the wet ground. They survived only by eating raw potatoes, since they couldn't light a fire for fear of being discovered. The local population was very hostile, and most of the peasants refused to help them. In her village, Jean's mother was terrified, fearing for her son's life. In spite of the brutal cold, she used to sleep without a blanket. "I want to feel what my son feels now, in the cold out there," she told her family.

Worse was to come. On November 13, 1943, the Resistance party was attacked by more than a hundred troops. Jean and a few comrades escaped, but they lost several men and all of their equipment.

Shortly thereafter, an urgent order from London reached the small group, now operating close to Issoudun, a market town in the Indre. The Resistance was short of funds, and they were assigned to attack the local branch of the Banque de France and send the money to London.

The complicity of the bank's security guards, two elderly men, was obtained beforehand. They offered token resistance, then obligingly collapsed on the floor. Jean and his friends ran to waiting cars, dragging heavy bags of money. The bags were then transferred to a van that Jean drove to a clearing in the forest close to the village of La Souterraine, where it was supposed to be picked up by another team. Jean was ordered to wait as long as it took, until the men from London came. "It will take only a couple of hours," his commander said.

Thus the young fighter found himself deep in the Creuse forest, in the middle of the night, with a van full of money. He had never seen such a fabulous treasure. He couldn't say how much money they had taken, perhaps 100 million francs. He waited until morning, but nobody came. Jean was worried, cold, tired, but most of all hungry. The hunger drove him crazy.

Finally he couldn't resist anymore. He opened the van's back door and took a 5,000-franc bill. He felt miserable taking this money, as if he were betraying the Resistance, but he was famished. He left the van, which was well hidden in the bushes, and walked to the nearest village. The baker's shop was open, filled with tantalizing smells. Jean walked in, asked for a loaf of bread, and produced the money. The burly baker examined the 5,000-

franc bill, then suspiciously eyed the skinny youngster. "Where did you get all this money, kid?" he inquired.

Jean thought, If you only knew . . .

The two men from London finally arrived at the meeting point, thirty-six hours late. Not bothering to say what had caused the delay, they got into the van and drove off. Jean walked eight miles through the forest, reached a country road, and rejoined his unit.

A few weeks later, on December 17, 1943, he was sent to Paris to join the Resistance commando unit that operated under the orders of the legendary colonels Morlot and Ravanel. He convinced his family to move back to Paris as well, using false ID papers. In the village where they lived, people knew they were the parents of "Jeannot the terrorist," and they could be arrested at any moment. Paris seemed safer now. "You'll have trouble getting on a train in the next few days, though," he said to his mother.

"How do you know?" she asked.

"I *should* know. I blew up the tracks last night."

At first the Parisian underground fighters didn't take the young man seriously. "If you want to join us, kid, you should bring your own weapon," they told him. Jean knew what that meant. "Bringing one's weapon" meant killing a German for it.

That night he took the hammer his father kept at home, sneaked into a military compound on the Boulevard des Sablons, and smashed in the head of a German sentry. He then brought the soldier's submachine gun to Resistance headquarters. The freedom fighters were impressed, and he was allowed to join the Groupe Franc National under the nom de guerre Jean Noël.

His young looks could be deceptive. Another leading

figure in the Resistance, Charles Gonnard, was alarmed
when he saw the skinny, curly-headed lad attending secret
meetings. "You must be crazy," he said to the Parisians.
"You're fighting the war with children now?" A few
weeks later, though, he changed his mind when he found
out that the "child" was a formidable fighter. Some of
Jeannot's friends even nicknamed him "the general."

Jean took part in some of the most daring operations
of his Paris unit. They bombed the plants of Air Liquide,
which supplied fuel for the German V-1 rockets, and of
Bronzavia, which specialized in ball bearings. They
bombed and partly destroyed the power plant at Chevilly-
Larue. They lobbed hand grenades into a Pigalle nightclub
frequented by the Gestapo, leaving a score of German
dead.

In one gratifying success, they raided the Commissariat Général du Travail Obligatoire—the compulsory-labor
department on the Place de Fontenoy—and set fire to the
records of all young Frenchmen slated for work in Germany. Vichy prime minister Pierre Laval, acting on Hitler's order, had decreed in September 1942 that every
French youth be sent to Germany to work for an unspecified period. The program amounted to a massive
conscription of slave labor for the Nazi war effort. The
young people lived in camps close to the plants where
they worked, and received pitiful wages, and almost
nobody was released before the end of the war. The
French administration had assembled detailed files on the
young men eligible to be sent to Germany in the years
1943–44. Following the sabotage by Jean and his comrades, the entire project had to be suspended for eighteen
months.

The team mounted operations against German soldiers

and officers, collaborators and traitors. A favorite tactic of Jean and his friends was to shoot German soldiers in Paris's public toilets. Once they attacked a police van transporting captured Resistance members to prison, freeing them and killing some of their guards.

Thus emboldened, Jean's group next attempted to rescue one of the Resistance leaders, Jean-Pierre Lévy, who was being interrogated at the Palais de Justice, the heavily guarded main court of Paris. Against overwhelming odds, the commando unit attacked his guards with submachine guns and grenades. They were repelled by heavy fire but managed to reach the waiting getaway cars. Jean-Pierre Lévy was rescued in another operation a few months later.

In early 1944 Jeannot helped to plan the kidnapping and court-martial of Philippe Henriot, the pro-Nazi propaganda minister of the Vichy government. The operation was undertaken in the spring, and Henriot was killed while resisting his attackers. But this was one raid Jean Frydman didn't take part in. A few weeks earlier, he had been captured by the Gestapo.

David Frydman would vividly remember the morning of May 3, 1944. At the time the family was living at 4 rue Martel, and Jean occasionally slept at home. Early that morning, French Gestapo agents broke into their apartment building and arrested Jean. Twelve-year-old David ran downstairs and saw the Gestapo agents massed outside. "They looked like ravens," he recalled, "dressed in black, running around and shouting, 'We've got him! We've got Jeannot!' "

Jean was taken to a building that inspired fear in every French heart: the rue des Saussaies headquarters of the French Gestapo. In the torture cellars of the Brigades Spéciales the nineteen-year-old was savagely beaten. His ribs were broken and his face smashed during long interrogations. Two weeks later he was handed over to the German authorities and jailed at Fresnes prison.

On July 9, Jean Frydman was taken to a drab building on rue Boissy-d'Anglas that had been requisitioned by the Wehrmacht. There he was tried by a German military court and sentenced to death. Then he was sent back to Fresnes to await execution.

He spent twenty-seven days in a solitary cell lit by a naked lightbulb hanging from the ceiling. A sadistic guard tormented him every day at dawn by rattling his keys and abruptly unlocking the cell door to make the youth believe he was going to die in a few minutes.

On the day set for Frydman's execution he was brought with a few other death-row prisoners to the inner court of the prison. But at the last moment a German SS officer, the notorious Sturmbannführer Alois Brünner, arrived and ordered a stay of execution. Eichmann's devoted assistant, Brünner was fanatically dedicated to the Final Solution. The year before, fresh from the annihilation of the Greek Jewish community, he had been named Eichmann's envoy to France, replacing Theodor Dannecker, who had sent 60,000 French Jews to their deaths. Now Brünner instructed the prison warden to separate Frydman from the other prisoners. He was a Jew, and Jews, Brünner said, were transported to Germany to die there.

The German officers in charge of Fresnes prison indignantly protested. They stressed that "Jeannot" was going to be shot anyway, so there was no reason to take him away. But Brünner doggedly overruled all objections. Even the fact that the Allies had landed in Normandy the month before and were already at the outskirts of Paris didn't influence his determination to send Jews to the gas chamber up to the very end.*

Awaiting his deportation, Frydman was transferred to Drancy, the notorious camp where scores of thousands of French Jews had been gathered before being taken to the death camps in Germany and Poland. Drancy had become a symbol not only of the French Jews' tragedy but also of the ugliest aspects of France's collaboration with the Nazis.

On August 17, 1944, Frydman boarded the last train leaving the Paris area for Germany. The train was a freight convoy to which Brünner's SS had attached a boxcar holding fifty-one prisoners, most of them Jewish Resistance members.

Most, but not all. Among the prisoners were also a Russian aristocrat, Princess Olga Galitzine; a rich and influential Jewish banker, Armand Kohn and his family (his mother at first refused to board the boxcar, insisting she always traveled first class); and the aeronautical engineer Marcel Bloch, who would retain his nom de guerre Marcel Dassault and become famous as the father of the Mirage supersonic aircraft. The story of this bizarre group, locked together in a cattle car on its way to the death camps, was described by a French writer, Jean-François Chaigneau, in his best-selling book *Le Dernier Wagon* (The Last Car).

From the recollections of the prisoners, Frydman, "the general," emerges as a wild, nervous, clever youngster who knew how to impose his will. His only concern was to organize the prisoners' escape from the train. Some of the prisoners refused to cooperate, viewing the risk as too

---

* After the war Brünner escaped to Syria, which offered him and other Nazis a cozy sanctuary. In the seventies he was blinded by a letter bomb sent by Jewish avengers. Some sources claim that the package was sent by agents of the Mossad.

great. Yet, together with some other Resistance members, using tools smuggled aboard, Frydman succeeded in breaking through the wooden floor of the car. Twenty-seven prisoners escaped from the slow-moving train in the early hours of August 21.

The escape was marked by a regrettable incident. Marcel Bloch, fearing that the Germans would massacre the prisoners who stayed aboard the train, tried to prevent the escape. He pounded on the boxcar's wall, hoping to attract the attention of the German guards. But Jean Frydman jumped on his throat. "If you do that again, you snitch, I'll kill you," he muttered. Bloch turned his face to the wall and kept quiet.

After the escape the Germans didn't shoot the remaining prisoners. But out of the twenty-four who remained in the car, nine perished in the death camps.

The escaped prisoners spread throughout the French countryside. One of them, Philippe Kohn, reached the city of Saint-Quentin, which was still occupied by the Germans. Ten days after the escape, U.S. Army tanks appeared at the city gates. Kohn, amazed, recognized the young man riding on the first tank, leading the liberators: Jean Frydman.

After the escape Frydman had crossed the German lines in search of advance units of the American forces. "The general" had used his favorite ruse for the last time in the war: he cut his trousers. As usual, the German sentries didn't bother to check the identity of the kid in short pants running through their lines.

A few weeks later, "the general" became Sublieutenant Jean Noël, the youngest officer in the French army.

The new officer returned to Paris in a crisp new uniform and high spirits. But his euphoria didn't last long.

His father greeted him with terrible news: his mother had been arrested by the Germans and deported to the concentration camps.

Jean was devastated. A special bond connected the mother and her older son. During the war her thoughts had been focused on him all the time. Whenever he managed to come home, she would bake him his favorite cake, with eggs and butter she bought for a fortune on the black market. She feared constantly that his Resistance activities would lead to his death. "Don't take such risks," she begged in tears. "We can hide, but you're too young to die."

Jean resolved to go to Germany and find her. A friend of his arranged for him to meet with the Secretary-General for Prisoners of War, a young man named François Mitterrand. Mitterrand appointed him a liaison officer with the British Eighth Army, and Jean left for Germany. In April 1945 he was transferred to a special unit handling the repatriation of prisoners from the concentration camps and traveled often back and forth to France. One night, when in Paris, he received a report about a convoy of French prisoners who had been taken from Auschwitz to Bergen-Belsen. Hoping his mother was among them, he drove to Brussels, where he succeeded in boarding a military aircraft bound for Germany.

The aircraft landed at the Lüneburg air base. It was surrounded by a crowd of excited Canadian soldiers. "Himmler!" they were shouting. "Himmler is here!"

Himmler? The chief of the SS? Frydman jumped in a jeep, which motored toward a bunker close to the runway.

In a small, dark room Jean found a short man, naked but for a pair of underpants, lying on an iron bed. His skin had a bluish tinge. The man had committed suicide a few hours before by swallowing a cyanide pill.

"I couldn't take my eyes off him," Jean wrote. "He was lying in front of me, dead, the creator of the Gestapo and the SS, and in my mind I clearly saw again the German hordes entering Paris five years before. For me, at this very moment, the circle was closed.

"I felt with absolute certitude that I had been right to do what I did, and that the Resistance was not only morally necessary but also the only realistic solution. And thanks to the Resistance I stood here now, a young veteran clad in the uniform of a victorious army, looking at my dead enemy, in his land ravaged by the Nazi ideology, to whose defeat my friends and I had contributed our share."

Jean Frydman finally reached Bergen-Belsen and discovered scenes of unspeakable horror. He saw the living skeletons that crawled out of the prisoners' barracks; he saw the piles of naked corpses that the British were shoving with bulldozers into mass graves. The terrible images of Bergen-Belsen would haunt him forever.

A few weeks later Jean's mother was found, alive, in Auschwitz. She too had become a living skeleton, but her spirit had not been broken. After the camp was liberated by the Red Army, she passed through Odessa and finally returned to Paris, to her husband and children.

Jean was stationed in Vienna when the war ended. Finally he could fulfill his dream. On a furlough from his unit, he put on his best uniform and traveled to Pau to find his beloved Angela.

But the Angel wasn't there. She had been taken away with her family by the Germans, her neighbors said.

Angela had died in Auschwitz.

3

In Paris in June 1989, Jean Frydman paid a visit to the Tribunal de Commerce to check Paravision's register. It had been recently modified, he found, with his name removed from the list of board members. Pietrini had acted swiftly, and Frydman's phony resignation had been duly certified.

When L'Oréal's executives heard about the dramatic confrontation between Frydman and Pietrini, and about Frydman's fury, they were not overly disturbed. "It was just a show. The man wants money," one of them said, contemptuously rubbing his thumb and forefinger. "Jean will always settle for money. We'll pay him a bundle for his stock and he'll quiet down."

They were wrong.

"My brother is a tough businessman," David Frydman later said. "He likes to succeed in his endeavors. He is always ready to make a good deal. But people can misjudge him. There are three things he regards as sacred: his family, Israel, and the Resistance. This time they had

hurt two of them—Israel, by the boycott, and his past as
a Resistance hero, by employing Corrèze. And he decided
to fight back."

"To understand why Jean Frydman became so totally
obsessed by this affair," a Paris judge, Jean-Pierre Getti,
explained, "one should know that the events of the war,
his struggle against the Nazis, were very vivid in his mind.
He couldn't let anybody spoil his memories. He had been
very deeply affected in mind and body by that period, and
all of a sudden he discovers that Corrèze is involved in
his ouster from L'Oréal, as if his conflict with the Nazis
hadn't ended.

"When he heard that Corrèze was behind his eviction,
he called Klarsfeld to find out who Corrèze is, and Klarsfeld said: 'But he is this notorious member of the
Cagoule!'

"That drove him crazy."

Jean Frydman, when he was discharged from the army
and returned to Paris in early 1946, was a happy man.
General de Gaulle, the savior of France, was prime minister. France had become, along with the United States,
Great Britain and the USSR, one of the four powers that
ruled the postwar world. The Vichy traitors had paid for
their crimes. Pierre Laval had been sentenced to death and
executed. Marshal Pétain had also been condemned to
death. True, General de Gaulle had commuted his sentence to life imprisonment, but he would die in his jail on
Yeu Island.

Jean's Resistance friends were now colonels, generals,
ministers. They were delighted to see him. He was invited
to many ceremonies, where he was kissed on both cheeks
by government dignitaries and army officers. He listened
to many speeches and was awarded many medals.

One day, however, the ceremonies were over and he had to find a job. For the following six years he worked in the small workshop of his father, who made and sold women's underwear. But he had other goals. He was fascinated by television. In 1952 he joined a group preparing a television network for Morocco. This was Telma, the first private television company to be created in Europe and Africa; all the rest were state controlled. In 1953 Frydman was appointed director of the company. When Telma collapsed because of political turmoil in Morocco, Frydman joined the Paris-based Thomson firm as adviser for television development. Four years later he was a founder of the Europe 1 radio station and the television station Télé Monte Carlo.

He soon became director general, then president, of Télé Monte Carlo, a commercial network broadcasting to France from neighboring Monaco. He had to beat all-powerful competition, the French government's television network, and he knew how he could do it—by broadcasting a different movie every night. But where could he get enough movies?

Inspired by a crazy idea, he flew to the United States, to Las Vegas. At the Desert Inn he had the most bizarre meeting in his life. While he sat on one side of a locked door, his interlocutor sat on the other. Mormon lackeys silently walked in and out of the room, bringing Jean pieces of paper sent by his invisible host. The man avoided any human contact, fearing a visitor might infect him with deadly germs. His name was . . . Howard Hughes.

Jean Frydman had heard the legends about the strange, reclusive millionaire, the man who had built a huge aircraft industry, who had owned RKO studios and managed TWA, who had been the lover of some of the most beautiful movie stars in Hollywood and the friend of politicians and statesmen. Frydman knew, though, that during recent years Hughes had been haunted by an eerie fear of microbes, had grown long hair and nails, and avoided all but his Mormon staff. Throughout the entire negotiation Jean Frydman didn't catch a glimpse of Hughes. They did, however, sign an agreement. Frydman acquired the European rights to the formidable RKO library of 740 movies controlled by Hughes. A few years later Frydman acquired the NTA (National Television Associates) library of 1,000 movies. Now he owned the rights to classics like *Citizen Kane*, *King Kong*, *Rio Grande*, *High Noon*, and the great Fred Astaire–Ginger Rogers musicals.

Frydman bought both libraries at bargain prices. At the time nobody believed that old movies, especially the antediluvian black-and-white films, were still of interest to anybody. But they became the key to Frydman's fortune. He later bought several collections of popular French movies, including some Jean Gabin classics, as well as 117 television series and movies, among them *Les Demoiselles d'Avignon*. Frydman also purchased the rights to other successful movies such as *L'Avventura* and *Gorky Park*, and hundreds of documentaries.

In France, Frydman was gradually acquiring a leading position in the world of cinema and broadcasting. Europe 1 grew to be France's most popular radio station. Jean's circle of acquaintance extended to influential politicians, movie stars, singers, and writers. Lino Ventura, Simone Signoret, and Yves Montand became his close friends.

Still, he continued to be haunted by his experience under the Nazi occupation. In the next decade he took part in producing several movies that profoundly marked the French national conscience, like the unforgettable

Marcel Ophüls documentary *The Sorrow and the Pity* (1970), which examined French conduct under the Nazis.

Frydman also produced a documentary about the Algerian war, *French People, If You Only Knew*, and later *Sakharov* and *From Nuremberg to Nuremberg*, a documentary movie in two parts telling the story of the rise and fall of Nazism. In 1969 he participated in the production of *Z*, the Costa-Gavras thriller about the military coup in Greece, starring Yves Montand.

While visiting Israel in 1962, he founded a company that introduced commercials to the state-owned radio. He had earlier met David Ben-Gurion, Moshe Dayan, and Shimon Peres during their visits to Paris; he had even helped Peres, the young director general of Israel's defense ministry, to establish his first contacts with several French political leaders in the mid-fifties. These contacts helped forge the French-Israeli alliance during the Suez war and the Sinai campaign in 1956.

Frydman's empire steadily expanded. In Paris, he created and presided over Médiavision, a company that produces and distributes commercials for movie theaters. In Canada, he acquired and developed a huge ranch near Calgary raising cattle and horses. Everything was going his way, for gas was later discovered on this property.

In 1967, during the Six-Day War, he went to Israel with a delegation of French Jews. Witnessing Israel's dramatic victories and visiting the Wailing Wall in Jerusalem, he felt an overwhelming attachment to the country and a deep identification with its people. He soon became a frequent visitor, and his circle of Israeli friends expanded.

One evening, as he arrived at the El Al counter at Orly airport to check in, he thought he saw the Angel. The young woman facing him looked exactly as he remembered Angela—the same heart-shaped face, honey blond hair, and blue eyes—except that she was wearing an El Al hostess uniform. He stared, stunned, as she approached him and introduced herself as Daniela, in charge of El Al's VIP service. He desperately wanted to talk to her. "Don't misunderstand me," he said. "I'm not trying to pick you up, but you remind me of my first love."

They struck up a conversation, and she told him she came from Israel and was studying publicity in Paris. "I can help you," he said. "I'm in advertising myself."

He gave her his phone number and hurried to the plane, his thoughts still dwelling on the young woman. He reminded himself he was a married man. But the marriage, his second, was falling apart and he was about to divorce. The meeting with Daniela had stirred him profoundly.

After Jean Frydman left the El Al counter, Daniela tore up the piece of paper on which he had scribbled his phone number and threw it in the garbage. She had no intention of calling him. She then got into her car and drove back to Paris. While she was driving, however, she changed her mind. She stopped at a gas station, called a friend who still was at Orly, and asked her to find the torn note with Frydman's number. Who knows? she thought. I might need a connection to the world of publicity.

Daniela called Jean several months later. They started meeting and fell in love. Two years later they were married, and they now have two daughters.

Their marriage had another salutary effect. For many years Jean had been cool and distant toward David, whose childhood admiration for his older brother remained intact. David held Jean's second wife responsible for the breach. He still longed for the family dinners on Saturday evening, when they all would gather around the table set by their mother. Everything changed, though, when Jean married Daniela. Radiating warmth and affection, the young woman brought Jean and David together. "Thanks to Daniela, we became brothers again," David Frydman said.

After bringing David into the film business, Jean Frydman built a house in Israel, and in the mid-eighties he applied for Israeli citizenship. Besides becoming a partner in several Israeli companies, he became a supporter of the Israeli Labor Party led by his close friend Shimon Peres.

And in 1988, Frydman became L'Oréal's partner in creating Paravision with his old friend François Dalle.

The partnership started well. A relaxed atmosphere reigned in their Champs-Élysées offices, a feeling of success and confidence. They were all movie people now, and behaved as such. They went to Cannes in May for the film festival, where they were invited to lavish parties and private screenings. "Our people got used to patting each other on the back," a former Paravision employee said archly, "and calling each other by their first names, and kissing on the mouth."

Those days ended, however, with Pietrini's revelations about Corrèze. The atmosphere in the elegant Paravision offices was irretrievably poisoned. David Frydman, feeling a deep empathy for his older brother, set out to help him. As ever, David didn't care about money. He was propelled rather by an insatiable curiosity and a passion for history. This fascination with his country's past transformed itself into a personal crusade to clear Jean's name as he started his search for material on Corrèze. His dedication was intensified by his feeling that the common battle brought him and Jean much closer.

After many years of living different, and sometimes distant, lives, the two brothers were now fighting together against the boycott and a war criminal. David considered both to be noble causes. Having read the Corrèze curriculum vitae that Daniela found, David started visiting libraries, archives, and research centers, and interviewing experts on World War II. Slowly, painstakingly, he established a file on Jacques Corrèze. Out of the documents and testimonies gathering on his desk, a strange, bloody story emerged.

4

Jacques Corrèze rose to prominence during a murky period in the history of France, more than a half century ago, when violent forces were plotting to smother the Republic.

It started in the mid-thirties, when iron-fisted dictatorships were emerging all over Europe. In Germany, Hitler seized power in 1933 and mesmerized an entire nation with visions of racial supremacy. Italy was already firmly behind the impetuous Mussolini. In the Spanish civil war, the republicans were fighting a losing battle against Franco's advancing columns.

In France, governments were forming and dissolving with dizzying rapidity. Traditional politicians were losing ground to the extremist right-wing movements that were sprouting in urban areas, preaching violence. Their principal enemies were the Communists and Socialists, who were on the rise as well. Huge rallies gathered under red banners in city squares; striking workers occupied factories or marched in the streets singing the "Internationale," deploying Marxist slogans, and raising their right fists in the Communist salute. The Socialists rallied behind the fiery, eloquent Léon Blum, who was not only a socialist but a Jew.

Groups of right-wing fanatics, some of them army officers, plotted violent ways to prevent the "reds" from taking power. In February 1936 Blum survived an assassination attempt by a group of dissident Action Française members led by a brutal killer named Jean Filliol. In the elections that followed three months later, the Left won, and Léon Blum became prime minister. He formed a coalition called the Popular Front, an alliance of left-wing parties and Communists. A few weeks later he dissolved the rightist extreme leagues.

French conservatives were desperate: they were convinced France was about to fall into the hands of the Communists. A group of fanatics led by a sinister, charismatic engineer, Eugène Deloncle, created the Secret Committee of Revolutionary Action, aimed at overthrowing the government. Deloncle was a stocky, dark-haired man with heavy jowls, a pugnacious chin, and cold brown eyes that could suddenly turn wild and threatening. He had been a seaman, an artillery officer, also a court-appointed expert witness in technical matters, but he was inexorably drawn to politics and violence. He used to say, "*Nous sommes méchants!*" We are evil!

One of the committee's backers was a brilliant chemist who specialized in soaps, lotions, and cosmetics. His name was Eugène Schueller.

At that time Schueller was in his late fifties. The son of a Parisian baker of Alsatian origins, the young man had worked in his father's shop, then earned his living as a street vendor while studying chemical engineering and pharmacology. In 1910 he invented a hair dye which he named L'Oréal. He later called his cosmetics company by the same name. Schueller then started a professional magazine for hairdressers, *La Coiffure de Paris*.

After World War I, in which he fought bravely, he was briefly associated with a Jew, Baron Henri de Rothschild. The result of their joint venture was a new soap, Monsavon. Schueller was tireless in his pursuit of success. He bought a paint factory, Valentine, invented a new shampoo, Dop, and started a second periodical, a women's magazine named *Votre Beauté*. Other lotions, dyes, creams, and soaps followed. Schueller soon became a rich man.

Being a tycoon was not enough, though. He also was strongly attracted to public and political life. Before the war he had joined a lodge of Freemasons, a secret order with a history dating back to the cathedral builders of the Middle Ages and a code based on morality, ethics, respect of the law of the land, and belief in a "supreme being" that could be the God of all religions. Not surprisingly, the Catholic Church and conservative political groups regarded the Freemasons with profound hostility.

As his fortune grew, Eugène Schueller's views gradually moved to the right and he began to repudiate old positions. In time he would see the Freemasons as an enemy of France. Having been the business associate of a Jew, he now became a virulent anti-Semite. Along the way he developed a simplistic economic theory about "proportional wages" in industry, according to which workers' wages would be made up of a base salary level and a proportional share of the company's profits. Schueller also advocated that workers and industry owners be grouped in professional corporations placed under state control; that, he said, would make the class struggle disappear. Such theories fitted to perfection the economic and social ideologies of the fascist regimes in Germany and Italy.

With the election of Léon Blum, Schueller was drawn to the most extremist circles, which preached "rather Hitler than the Popular Front." Mesmerized by the violent personality of Eugène Deloncle, Schueller opened his Paris offices and his purse to Deloncle—and he became actively involved in Deloncle's Secret Committee of Revolutionary Action. Many of the committee meetings took place at L'Oréal's headquarters at 14 rue Royale.

The committee became known as La Cagoule—the Cowl—because of the blood red hoods its leaders wore at its secret meetings to conceal their identities. "I swear to keep the secret," whispered Cagoule members facing their red-hooded, white-gloved leaders, "and I'll never try to discover the identity of my chiefs."

Deloncle's identity was well known, though, to a young furniture salesman from Auxerre. When Deloncle and his wife were furnishing their country mansion, they visited the store where he worked. Deloncle took a liking to the handsome salesman and invited him to come to Paris. A former member of the right-wing group Les Camelots du Roi, the young man had been disappointed by their inaction. He was tall, slim, dark-haired, and violent, yet a charming man and a born leader. In Paris he became Deloncle's faithful assistant and confidant. Living in his home, he fell deeply in love with Deloncle's stunning wife, Mercedes. Years later he would claim that it was because of his "crazy love" for her that he had followed the couple to Paris. The young man was twenty-four years old when La Cagoule was born. His name was Jacques Corrèze.

Corrèze became involved in many of the bloody activities carried out by La Cagoule in the tumultuous years preceding World War II. His underground name was La Bûche, the log, derived from the store Le Bûcheron—The Lumberjack—where he had worked. He was devoted to Eugène Deloncle, although some of his friends suspected him of being the lover of Deloncle's wife. His enemies among the Cagoulards also used to say that he was an uneducated man with no principles.

For a while Corrèze was in charge of swearing-in ceremonies, shooting practice, and the group's weapons caches. La Cagoule accumulated huge quantities of arms and explosives, meant to be used in a coup against the Republic. In Paris alone, one of their depots held 7,740 hand grenades, 34 machine guns, 400 rifles, and hundreds of thousands of rounds of ammunition.

In 1937, soon after its creation, La Cagoule carried out a dozen political assassinations. Cagoule saboteurs blew up four aircraft that were on their way to Republican Spain. In Paris they sabotaged buildings belonging to the Union of Industry Owners in an effort to frame the Communists, who were in bitter dispute with the industrialists. Cagoule activists also established an armored cell and a torture chamber in the cellar of a Rueil villa, where they hoped to torture the prime minister Léon Blum and other leaders of the French Republic after carrying out their coup d'état. They even stole lethal poisons from research institutes in order to assassinate traitors and chosen enemies; the poisons were never used, however.

The most spectacular exploit of La Cagoule was the 1937 assassination of two Italian antifascists, the brothers Carlo and Nello Rosselli. Carlo Rosselli, a man devoted to democracy, had planned the escape of an important socialist leader from Italy. He had been arrested by Mussolini's fascist police, sentenced to five years in prison, and deported to the Lipari Islands. Rosselli escaped from the islands, however, crossed the French border and reached Paris, where he founded a dissident newspaper, *Giustizia e Libertà*.

The SIM, Mussolini's secret service, asked La Cagoule to liquidate Rosselli, offering in return several crates of Beretta machine guns. Corrèze, as Deloncle's assistant, personally ordered the murder. A group of Cagoulards, led by the same Filliol who had tried the year before to assassinate Léon Blum, ambushed a car carrying Carlo and his seventeen-year-old brother, Nello, near Bagnoles-de-l'Orne. They savagely butchered the Italians with guns and knives, for the use of a knife was the ritual "signature" of La Cagoule.

In November 1937, La Cagoule attempted its long-planned coup against the regime. The pretext for their armed uprising was an imaginary Communist plot to seize power in the country; in this situation La Cagoule could benefit from the support of the right wing and "save France" from the "reds." Deloncle and his men established secret command posts and prepared maps of Paris, assigning strategic objectives to each of their units. Corrèze's role was to carry out the attack on the Ministry of Postal Services. But the coup failed and Deloncle was arrested. Many Cagoule leaders, including Corrèze, fled to Spain. Corrèze, now the organization's secretary general, arrived in Spain artfully disguised, wearing glasses and a blond beard, with his dark hair also dyed blond.

When he returned to Paris the following year, he claimed his purpose was to rescue Deloncle. However, many of his friends believed he had come back to see his mistress, the beguiling Mercedes Deloncle. In any case, he was arrested and thrown in prison along with her husband.

In 1940, Corrèze was offered a release if he joined

the French army. He accepted, and participated in France's unsuccessful fight against the German blitzkrieg. The commander of his regiment, ironically, was Charles de Gaulle.

With the humiliating defeat of France, La Cagoule broke into three groups. One crossed the English Channel and joined de Gaulle in London. A second faction swore allegiance to Vichy. The third, the most extremist, chose to work directly with the Germans. Deloncle and Corrèze were among the leaders of the last group.

Deloncle finally had no need for subterfuge. Soon after the Wehrmacht occupied Paris, he created the "legal Cagoule." That was how he described the Mouvement Social Révolutionnaire (MSR), which immediately developed close ties with the Gestapo and the SS.

Corrèze and Filliol became members of MSR's political bureau, as did the millionaire Eugène Schueller, Deloncle's close friend. Their names appeared together on MSR posters, invitations, appeals, and flyers. Their first manifesto, entitled "Revolution! MSR Resurrection!" was signed by Schueller, Deloncle, and Corrèze, among others. An official document published by the MSR described the functions of its main leaders:

Chief: EUGÈNE DELONCLE
Deputy and substitute to the chief: JEAN FONTENOY
President and director of all the technical committees
    and study committees: SCHUELLER
Intelligence service: FILLIOL
Paris region: CORRÈZE
             CHARBONNEAU
Territorial organization: FAURAN

Corrèze joined another organization as well, La Communauté Française, which had its headquarters on rue Lord Byron, near the Champs-Élysées. The manifesto of this "French Community," which was signed by Corrèze and Filliol, among others, stated:

> The Jew, destroyer of any established order, alien to all faiths as well as to all territories, brought Corruption all over France.
>
> The Freemason powerfully helped the Jew in this task, by practicing everywhere an odious dictatorship.
>
> Therefore it is important . . . to cleanse our country, freeing it completely from these ferments of corruption and disintegration that are the Jews and the Freemasons.

With the blessings of the German embassy, the MSR published its platform, which was violently racist, anti-Semitic, and antidemocratic. It soon merged with another pro-Nazi movement headed by Marcel Déat, creating the Rassemblement National Populaire (RNP), whose secretary general in Paris was Jacques Corrèze.

The RNP platform declared: "Our aim is . . . to obtain the exclusion of the Jews from the life and the economy of France and protect the interests of the French who have been hurt by the Jews." At a huge RNP rally in June 1941, the speakers urged their fellow Frenchmen to "clean the country of the Jews and of their last natural child, Gaullism."

Schueller, the chief of the RNP technical committees, spoke of "the three revolutions": wages, management, and capital. To bring these revolutions about, the fiery Schueller expounded from his pulpit, "Right away, fifty or a hundred prominent people must be shot."

Huge RNP posters proclaimed from the walls of Paris: "The RNP frees the Frenchmen from their eternal masters—the Jews, the Freemasons, the members of Parliament." The posters also attacked the Vichy government, which seemed too mild to the fanatic Cagoule veterans: "Vichy revives the stupidities and crimes of the Parliament. Vichy is the refuge of the Jews and the Freemason Internationale."

The Cagoule veterans continued their bloody practices, using murder to settle accounts with their former enemies. In July 1941, they planted a bomb under the bed of former interior minister Marx Dormoy, who had exposed one of their plots in 1938. The explosion tore him to pieces.

Soon their brutal crimes gained new scope. On one night in October 1941, Deloncle and his friends blew up seven Paris synagogues. Ironically, there were no civilian casualties, but two Wehrmacht soldiers were killed. Following these bombings the chief of the Gestapo and the SD (Sicherheitsdienst, the SS intelligence service), Reinhard Heydrich, wrote to the incensed Wehrmacht General Staff:

> During the combat that [the French nation] is waging against international Jewry, my service has entered into contact with the French anti-Semitic organizations. For a long time, the anti-Semitic group of Deloncle was known as the most active of these groups, and Deloncle himself, in spite of his equivocal political character, offered the best guarantees for a merciless combat against the Jews. Deloncle also made it known that he was ready to carry out reprisal actions against the Jews. I accepted his offer only at the moment when the Jews . . . were charged with all the

crimes in Europe and were destined to definitely disappear from Europe.

The bombings carried out during the night against the seven Parisian synagogues showed that France, which used to be the European citadel of the Jews, could offer them security no longer.

Heydrich's letter was written on November 6, 1941. Two weeks later, on November 23, hundreds of MSR activists attended a huge rally in Paris to hear Deloncle before he went on a tour of the eastern front.

Members of the political bureau sat on the dais, and behind it, covering an entire wall, was painted the MSR logo: a white sword on a red and blue background, and under it the movement's slogan, *"Aime et sert"*—Love and Serve.

Schueller gave another fiery speech for the occasion: "What matters for us is a full and final severance from the recent past, from the methods and the men of the Third Republic, from Freemasonry and Jewry."

When the Final Solution was applied in France two years later, former Cagoule and MSR militants would willingly help the Vichy police chief René Bousquet, who rounded up sixty thousand Jews and handed them over to the Nazis for deportation to the death camps.

In the meantime, Jacques Corrèze was vigorously climbing the ladder of power. In March 1941, he joined the paramilitary arm of the RNP, the Légion Nationale Populaire, and was appointed territorial chief for Paris and its suburbs. He wore a black beret, high leather boots, and a dashing uniform with five stripes that gave him the rank of colonel. He was put in charge of six brigades of French fascists and participated in several anti-Jewish operations.

He didn't participate in the bombing of the synagogues, though, because by then he was engaged in a more devoted service to Hitler.

In September 1941, Corrèze gave the ultimate proof of his obedience to the Reich: he joined the Legion of French Volunteers (LVF) of the German army and swore allegiance to the Führer. He was also proving his obedience to Eugène Deloncle, who wanted to have a reliable representative in the LVF.

Corrèze first recruited French volunteers for the Legion, using recruitment offices located in stores confiscated from Parisian Jews. Corrèze then volunteered for the Russian front, obtained the rank of *Leutnant*, and commanded a squad of the Seventh Company, Second Battalion, 638th Infantry Regiment. In bitter cold weather (forty-five degrees below zero) he reached the outskirts of Moscow. When the Germans failed to breach the Russian front, he said later, he understood that "we were done." After a short stint on the front lines he was discharged and returned to France in April 1942.

While he was away, the political landscape had changed. There were persistent rumors that Deloncle had been the organizer of an assassination attempt on August 27, 1941, against Vichy prime minister Pierre Laval, who was shot and wounded. Bloody vendettas had erupted between Deloncle and other pro-Nazi leaders at the RNP. Deloncle was cast as a leper, and Eugène Schueller was among the first to break with his former hero. On March 18, 1942, Schueller visited the German embassy, where he proclaimed his loyalty to Hitler, who was in his eyes *"Führer Europas"*—the Leader of Europe. He also informed his Nazi friends that he wasn't supporting Deloncle anymore. Schueller's statements were noted by the embassy staff and duly reported to Berlin. He later said that he had decided to part ways with Deloncle after the Cagoule chief had deserted Marshal Pétain for being too soft.

In the spring of 1942, when Deloncle was ousted from his position, Corrèze loyally followed him. "I am not the kind that runs away," he said after the war. He would remain with Deloncle to the end.

Looking for a new protector, Deloncle tried to associate himself with the Gestapo, then turned toward the Abwehr, the German counterintelligence service. At dawn on January 7, 1944, in a shady settlement of accounts between the German secret services and their French associates, Deloncle was murdered in his Paris apartment on rue Le Sueur. His son, his wife, and Jacques Corrèze were in the apartment at the time. Deloncle's son was hit by a bullet and paralyzed for life. Corrèze was more fortunate. He dived under a table and wasn't hurt. The police report mentioned that he was found "naked in the hall."

Corrèze stayed with Mercedes Deloncle. According to some sources, he emerged later in 1944 at the Deloncle country house in Villers-Cotterêts, where he briefly hosted some pro-Nazi French leaders who were fleeing to Germany. At the liberation of France he was arrested at the Anthéor viaduct, close to the Italian border, in the company of fascist Milice paratroopers. These men had been trained in Germany and dropped into France to sabotage strategic installations. Corrèze's men intended to blow up the viaduct, cutting off one of the main roads connecting France and Italy. Ironically, this was exactly the same viaduct that Jean Frydman and his Resistance comrades had tried to blow up in 1942.

Corrèze was brought to trial for his Cagoule activities. The trial ran from October 11, 1948, to the end of November. Forty former members of La Cagoule crammed the benches in the defendants' box. Corrèze was in the first row, dressed in a suit and tie. By this time he had already spent three years in jail awaiting trial. While witnesses paraded before him, he watched with indifference. A Paris reporter wrote that he was "napping, displaying a total lack of interest in the proceedings." When he was asked about his part in the murder of the Rosselli brothers, he calmly replied that he had been mistaken for somebody else with a similar name, his friend Aristide Corre, the so-called Dagore.

The verdicts, announced after two months, were lenient, influenced by the atmosphere of national reconciliation that prevailed in France at the time. Only some escaped Cagoule killers, who were tried in absentia, were sentenced to death. Eleven extremists were acquitted, and most of the accused received suspended sentences. Corrèze, one of the ten Cagoulards whose crimes were judged serious enough to justify jail sentences, was given ten years in prison, and another ten years for his service in the Legion of French Volunteers, the sentences to be served concurrently. However, Corrèze was never tried for his Nazi activities in France during the war.

In the spirit of forgiveness that gradually pervaded France, the sentences of the Cagoulards were soon reduced. In 1950, after serving only two years, Corrèze was released. A court ruled that these two years, added to the time Corrèze had already spent in jail before the trial, amounted to five years, and he should be set free. Corrèze married Mercedes Deloncle and vanished.

Forty years later, he had emerged from the past, a rich, powerful resident of New York who owned homes in the Bahamas and Paris. He had become president of Cosmair, chairman of Helena Rubinstein cosmetics, and L'Oréal's main negotiator with the Arabs on the matter of the boycott against Israel.

How had the former Cagoule activist and Nazi criminal reached that position? The man who hired him initially was François Dalle, L'Oréal's president-to-be. "He just came to see me in 1950," Dalle said. "He was out of work, he had been recently released from prison, so we found him a job." To *Le Monde* he declared: "I don't exclude the excluded. He had paid [for his crimes]." In an interview with a Parisian magazine Dalle added: "It was a salesman's position, a shit job."

That was only partly true. Corrèze had not chosen L'Oréal blindly, but had come for help to his former friend and supporter, Eugène Schueller. By this time the founder of L'Oréal was one of the richest men in France.

It is unclear if Schueller helped Corrèze willingly, or if Corrèze blackmailed him into doing so. But there can be no doubt that Schueller personally found Corrèze a job at L'Oréal. The "salesman with the shit job" was soon sent to Spain and, following pressure from Paris, was appointed vice president of Procasa, the Spanish subsidiary of L'Oréal. He then moved to South America, where he worked for the local L'Oréal branches. He finally arrived in New York and shortly thereafter was appointed president of the newly formed Cosmair, L'Oréal's exclusive agent in the United States. All the while, Corrèze kept his apartment in Paris, and on November 28, 1966, he was fully rehabilitated by a French court.

In New York, in the course of promoting L'Oréal's products, Corrèze met hundreds of Jewish hairdressers and beauty salon managers. "With his small suitcase, he visited all the New York salons, to sell our hair dyes," François Dalle recalled. The hairdressers had no idea that the suave gentleman who worked so hard to sell them lotions and shampoos had once been a merciless Nazi.

Corrèze transformed Cosmair into a huge company, with revenues of $1 billion a year. In 1984, Nestlé bought 70 percent of Cosmair, with 26 percent remaining in the hands of Liliane Bettencourt, Schueller's daughter; L'Oréal's share shrank to a mere 4 percent.

Corrèze also met Helena Rubinstein, from whom he artfully concealed his past. The former Cagoule member and the stout Jewish tycoon became good friends. In the two decades following her death in 1965 he deftly used straw people and front firms to buy her company discreetly, acting for L'Oréal. When the deal was finally completed, he became president of the firm.

Corrèze, a fervent anti-Semite, was now president of a company bearing the name of a Zionist. Not only that, he was very proud of his acquisition. He proceeded to gradually discard the cheap mass-market Helena Rubinstein products and concentrate on a few high-quality items. He planned to transform Helena Rubinstein into a prestigious line of cosmetic products.

So when the Arab League decided in 1989 to boycott L'Oréal because of Helena Rubinstein's links with Israel, Corrèze was determined not to let that happen. He traveled back to France to organize L'Oréal's response to the Arab initiative. He was going to find a way for both L'Oréal and Helena Rubinstein to avoid the boycott.

5

The situation was so absurd that it seemed borrowed from a third-rate movie. Jean Frydman's partners had faked his resignation in order to yield to the Arab boycott. They had done so under the direction of a former Nazi who had immigrated to the United States, created an empire, and bought the company of a rich Jewess. Frydman realized he couldn't remain associated with L'Oréal anymore.

At the end of June, he met with François Dalle and made it clear how furious he was about the plot to make him resign. Moreover, he demanded to know why a respectable company like L'Oréal would employ Jacques Corrèze, a notorious Nazi criminal.

Dalle was conciliatory. Corrèze had come to L'Oréal after his release from prison, he said, and asked for a job. There was no reason not to employ him. After all, the man had paid for his crimes.

As for Frydman's resignation from Paravision, Dalle

claimed that the entire incident had been a misunderstanding. He reminded Jean Frydman of their dinner in Marbella a few days before the meeting of the strategic committee in Paris. During that dinner, Dalle said, he had spoken to Frydman about the problem of the boycott, and at that point Frydman had agreed to resign from Paravision.

Frydman denied this. During the entire evening in Marbella, they had never discussed business, he said. The Arab boycott and his resignation had been mentioned for the first time at the strategic committee meeting, out of the blue, and that had happened five days after the fake board meeting at which Frydman had allegedly resigned. He couldn't understand why his resignation had been faked and predated when he had made clear his refusal to leave Paravision.

"I refused to resign then," Frydman told Dalle. "But now, after finding out that you employ people like this Corrèze, I don't want to have anything more to do with L'Oréal. I'll sell you my Paravision stock and quit."

To Frydman's surprise, Dalle tried to dissuade him, and offered to reinstate him officially in his former functions as a member of the Paravision board. Frydman flatly refused.

Still, he couldn't help wondering what had caused Dalle's change of heart. Dalle had been quite worried back in April about Frydman's presence on the board. Why did he want him back now?

The truth was, Dalle knew something that Frydman didn't: the secret negotiations of L'Oréal with the Arab Boycott Bureau had reached a decisive stage, and good news from Damascus could be expected at any moment. It arrived indeed on July 5. L'Oréal's envoy to the Middle

East flashed a jubilant telex message to the Centre Schueller: HIP HIP HOURRA—L'OREAL EST SORTI DU BOYCOTT!

He added: "Later in the day we'll transmit to you our orders [for cosmetic products] for Syria and Jordan."

With the lifting of the boycott, Dalle apparently saw no reason why Frydman should be persona non grata anymore on the Paravision board of directors. In his view, it was time to bury the hatchet.

In spite of Frydman's indignant refusal, the bosses of L'Oréal decided to make a last effort to bring him back. A meeting of the board, a real one this time, was convened on October 16, 1989, with the intention of reappointing Jean Frydman to his former position. The members of the board were invited by personal letter.

The board met in the Paravision conference room at the Champs-Élysées headquarters. François Dalle, Michel Pietrini, Jean-Pierre Meyers, and a L'Oréal lawyer attended the meeting. The brothers Frydman had been invited, as if nothing had happened. But Jean Frydman did not attend; his brother David came alone. David was a deceptively soft-spoken man, but behind his pleasant smile was the tenacity of a bulldog. As the meeting started, he raised his hand and asked to read a written declaration:

> I solemnly protest against certain allegations . . . in the written account of the board of directors that allegedly took place on March 30, 1989.
>
> 1. It is written that Mr. Jean Frydman signed the attendance sheet of that meeting. This is false.
>
> 2. It is written that he signed a letter of resignation from his position as member of the board. This is false.

3. It is written that I personally signed the attendance sheet. This is false.

Concerning this third point, you'll understand, gentlemen, that I consider it outrageous that anybody on this board might imagine that I would become an accomplice, even by keeping silent, of a discriminatory measure which led to the ouster of my brother for the sole reason that he is a French citizen residing in Israel.

I feel outraged precisely because the matter at hand concerns my own brother, because I am Jewish, and finally because, as a French citizen respecting the laws of my country, I know that they prohibit racial discrimination and forbid [commercial] enterprises to yield to the menaces of boycott practiced by certain foreign governments.

David Frydman's letter ended by rejecting the proposed reinstatement of his brother. "I consider the present meeting as an attempt to erase the facts and consequences regarding the fraudulent ouster of my brother. . . . I shall not be part of this camouflage in any way." In concluding, he asked that his letter be appended to the minutes of the meeting.

As soon as he had finished speaking, Michel Pietrini, Paravision's president, made a strange comment. He wanted to make clear, he said, that at its meeting of March 30, 1989, the board of directors had accepted the resignation of Jean Frydman. Pietrini's version was immediately corroborated by other board members representing L'Oréal.

David Frydman was indignant. All the people present, and above all Pietrini, knew perfectly well that there had been no meeting of the board on March 30. They all knew

Frydman couldn't have resigned at a meeting that never took place. By their statements they were trying to cover themselves in case any future legal action was taken. Once that had been done, they sweetly invited his brother to resume his seat on the board. That was hypocrisy at its worst. David Frydman angrily objected once again to the motion to reinstate his brother.

A heated discussion followed. Dalle protested Frydman's accusations and said he had never been an anti-Semite.

"I never accused you of anti-Semitism," David Frydman said.

Pietrini described his sympathy with Israel, noting that his children had worked on a kibbutz. "We have yielded to the boycott not because of racial prejudice, but for economic reasons."

David Frydman said that this argument only confirmed his accusations. His brother had been fraudulently removed because of L'Oréal's determination to comply with the boycott demands. Equally reprehensible, he said, the entire operation had been directed by a Nazi criminal named Corrèze.

"Corrèze?" Dalle said. "He's nothing but one small former collaborator among thirty thousand people who work for L'Oréal." Both Pietrini and Dalle maintained that Corrèze had nothing to do with the boycott affair.

When Frydman mentioned his brother's activities in the Resistance, Dalle angrily interrupted him. "Your brother wasn't the only resistant, you know," he said, showing the Resistance pin he was wearing under his lapel.

Frydman fired back, reminding Dalle that he had been implicated in a financial scandal quite recently. In a case of alleged insider trading of Société Générale bank shares, those involved included François Dalle and his wife.

Jean-Pierre Meyers turned to him. "You speak of moral principles," he said, "but you are thinking of a huge settlement."

When the shouting subsided, Pietrini presented two motions to the board. One, that the board recognize that Jean Frydman hadn't resigned. Two, that the board reinstate Jean Frydman in his functions retroactively.

Again David Frydman furiously objected. "I refuse to be associated with this cover-up," he declared.

The meeting finally ended without reaching a decision. It was agreed that another meeting of the board would be called shortly. But no further meeting ever took place.

The Frydman brothers stayed on at Paravision until the late fall to close a deal with the American film company Carolco for the purchase of several movies it had produced, a negotiation that Jean Frydman had begun before the eruption of the crisis. That was the Frydman brothers' last act as Paravision associates. Then they left the offices on the Champs-Élysées.

David Frydman revived his company, Ariès, and Jean Frydman used his brother's offices, because as a foreign resident he didn't have the right to own a business in France. He therefore operated through his Israeli and Dutch companies.

The legal conflicts between the Frydman brothers and L'Oréal began the same fall. On October 20, 1989, a meeting was convened between the Frydmans and L'Oréal in the presence of their lawyers, Bernard Gorny and Jean-Marie Degueldre respectively. L'Oréal was represented by Bettencourt's son-in-law, Jean-Pierre Meyers. Jean Frydman noticed that day and at several future meetings that L'Oréal sent Jewish executives or advisers to negotiate with him, probably in order to subtly make the point that there was no anti-Jewish discrimination in the company.

"I have made a mistake," Jean Frydman said, "by mixing two problems: a moral one, the boycott and Corrèze, and a financial one, the resolution of the dispute that has arisen between us inside Paravision." Frydman stressed that the two issues were totally separate. As far as the first was concerned, he was going to fight with all his heart, no matter what the solution of the second was. He explained that fighting the boycott and the former Nazis was for him essential, a duty. On this subject nothing was negotiable, and no compromise possible.

Frydman went on to say that in the matter of Paravision, on the other hand, there was no other solution but a divorce. "I'll do everything so that this divorce will take place in the most civilized conditions, and I am ready to consider your point of view."

Meyers and Frydman recognized that first they had to reach agreement on Paravision's market value. To do this they would appoint an arbiter to establish the value of Paravision's stock and consequently of the Frydmans' share. Frydman recalled that during a luncheon with François Dalle in September 1989, the older man had estimated the net value of Paravision at two billion francs (at the exchange rate then prevailing, roughly $315 million). Frydman had contested that estimate; he believed Paravision was worth between 2.5 and 3 billion francs ($400–$475 million).

The arbiter chosen by the two parties was André Rousselet, the president of the pay-television network Canal Plus. One of L'Oréal's lawyers suggested that a well-known banker, Jacques Mayoux, be appointed as his alternate, to which Frydman agreed.

At the end of this meeting, Frydman warned that he intended to sue L'Oréal for racial discrimination as soon as the arbiter submitted his final report. He didn't want to do that right away, he added, since he preferred to avoid mixing business with matters of principle.

Yet it seems that L'Oréal's representatives failed to understand Frydman's position. They knew he was a tough businessman who wouldn't refuse a good deal. They thought all he wanted was money and viewed the dispute with him essentially as a financial one. They believed he was using the boycott affair and the Corrèze involvement merely as levers in his effort to obtain a large compensation from L'Oréal.

For the former Resistance hero, though, the affair would become an obsession. He had been wounded to the core, and he was going to pursue his crusade against the boycott and Corrèze at all costs. Had L'Oréal's leaders paid better attention, they might have behaved differently.

In November, André Rousselet informed both sides that he couldn't pursue his work as arbiter because of a conflict of interest. He had become engaged in a negotiation to buy some of the Paravision stock, and he feared this might affect his objectivity. L'Oréal's lawyers suggested that he be replaced by his alternate, Jacques Mayoux, former president of the Société Générale, the second largest bank in France.

Frydman had no objection. The atmosphere was more relaxed now, and in January 1990 he even handed L'Oréal's attorney a letter of resignation from Paravision. This was the first time he formally stated, in writing, that he was quitting the company. The text of the letter had been agreed to by both sides. It was dated January 10, 1990, but certified that Frydman's resignation was in effect from April 1, 1989.

The financial disagreement was about to be resolved, after all. Frydman met Jacques Mayoux and came back very favorably impressed. He couldn't know that Mayoux's "expert appraisal" would spark another ugly episode in the Frydmans' confrontation with L'Oréal.

Jacques Mayoux was a prestigious banker whom François Mitterrand had described as "a man of great quality." Yet after a few months the Frydman brothers started to suspect that something was wrong. In the second half of June, Paravision's comptroller, Charles Leguide, called David Frydman. He wanted to warn him, Leguide said, that Mayoux was behaving very strangely. He was rejecting every piece of evidence that was in the Frydmans' favor; he had impatiently brushed off the comptroller's reports and his findings. Leguide felt that Mayoux was not acting as the impartial expert he was supposed to be.

David telephoned his brother. Worried, Jean Frydman came back from Israel. On June 25, 1990, he visited one of his lawyers, Michel Jobert, a well-known political figure and former cabinet minister who had only recently started a new career as an attorney. Frydman had known Jobert for forty-five years, since the immediate postwar period when both of them, young officers in the French army, had been stationed in Vienna. A thin, taciturn man with a rather unusual sense of humor, Jobert was a somewhat controversial figure in Paris. He wasn't popular in Jewish circles either, because of his harsh criticism of Israel.

As Frydman set forth his worries about Mayoux, Jobert looked at him, surprised. "Mayoux? Jacques Mayoux? He is your expert?"

"Yes," Frydman said, puzzled. "Why, what is wrong?"

"Do you know who he is?"

"Of course. He is the honorary president of the Société Générale."

Jobert walked over to a bookcase and picked up *Who's Who in France*. He leafed through the thick volume until he found the entry "Mayoux, Jacques."

Frydman perused the impressive biography. Mayoux was indeed a top-notch financial expert. Besides his position at the prestigious Société Générale, he was president of several major financial and industrial companies, and vice chairman of Goldman-Sachs Europe. If that wasn't enough, he had a seat on the board of another dozen or so companies and was a professor at the University of Paris. He had also been decorated with the Légion d'Honneur and other French and foreign medals.

But as Frydman reached the end of the entry, he suddenly froze. One of the last lines read: "Adviser to the Director of L'Oréal–Finances."

Jobert saw the pallor that spread on Frydman's face. The "impartial" expert had been, and perhaps still was, on L'Oréal's payroll!

A quick inquiry confirmed the conflict of interest: Mayoux had been employed by L'Oréal until the end of 1989 as a consultant, and had been paid for his services 125,000 francs (more than $20,000) every quarter. That represented an honorarium of $80,000–$90,000 a year. What's more, when he had accepted the appointment as an expert, he still was receiving disbursements from L'Oréal! He hadn't informed Frydman of that, although by French law he was explicitly required to do so.

Clearly, Frydman had to withdraw his agreement to Mayoux's appointment—and quickly. It was June 25, and Mayoux was supposed to deliver his report to the court by June 30. Jobert immediately sent a letter to Mayoux, asking him to resign his position. He stated the reasons for his demand: the links between Mayoux and L'Oréal. Mayoux, however, answered the following day that there was no "existing link" between him and L'Oréal, and therefore he saw no reason to resign.

Frydman and Jobert requested an urgent session of the court in order to cancel Mayoux's appointment. They virtually bombarded Mayoux and the L'Oréal lawyers with legal papers, faxes, and messenger-delivered letters. Mayoux didn't respond. They finally succeeded in forcing him to appear for a summary proceeding on June 29. Frydman and Jobert asked the court to relieve Mayoux of his functions. But to their dismay, Mayoux informed the court that he had already sent his report by registered letter on June 28. This meant it was too late for the court to act. As for Frydman's complaint, Mayoux claimed that he hadn't worked for L'Oréal since 1988, which of course wasn't true.

The court had no choice but to bow to the facts. Mayoux had delivered his report before the court session. He couldn't be removed from a job he had already completed.

Mayoux then distributed copies of his report to those present at the court session. The assessment was devastating. Mayoux estimated the value of Frydman's share in Paravision at 325 million francs—about $51 million. That estimate was lower by $30–50 million than the Frydman brothers' claim. It was even lower than an internal estimate made by L'Oréal's experts.

A case of collusion seemed all but proven.

At the risk of anticipating, it may be noted that almost

a year later a strange document was discovered in the archives of L'Oréal. Dated June 13, 1990, it was marked "Confidential" and was sent by Pierre Castres Saint-Martin, corporate financial director, to L'Oréal president Lindsay Owen-Jones and to the vice president for financial affairs, Marc Ladreit de Lacharrière. The subject of the letter was the acquisition of the Paravision stock from the Frydman brothers. It stated: "The price we'll have to pay for the Paravision stock will be established by Mr. Mayoux by June 30. We'll execute the operation as soon as Mr. Mayoux has established the value. We should anticipate that L'Oréal will have to pay 300 million francs for this acquisition, perhaps even more. . . ."

This letter is puzzling. How could Castres Saint-Martin know, seventeen days in advance, that Jacques Mayoux was going to establish the value of Frydman's stock at 300 million francs, perhaps more?

After his court victory, Mayoux ran into Michel Jobert in the parking garage. To Jobert he looked "superb, relaxed, full of disdain."

"You doubted my word," Mayoux said.

"It's up to you to put me back on the right track," Jobert answered, meaning that Mayoux had to prove that he had been right and that Jobert and his client had erred.

But it was the extraordinary gift of a young woman that put everybody back on the right track.

In their office the Frydman brothers, despondent, read Mayoux's report. It was dated June 27, 1990. Under the letterhead "Jacques Mayoux, 63 boulevard Haussmann, 75008 Paris," the document bore the title "Establishment of the Value of the Participation of the Frydman Group in the Assets Held by Paravision and Its Direct and Indirect Affiliates."

By chance, Catherine Morisse walked into the room at this moment. Morisse had stayed at Paravision after the Frydman brothers left, and in January 1990 she had been promoted to director of the administrative and legal services of Paravision. But she didn't feel comfortable about her role. One day Michael Stevens, who was her friend and a member of the board, came to see her. "Be careful," he said, "they don't trust you." Apparently the new team at Paravision were suspicious of her close ties with Jean Frydman. She therefore decided to quit her job. Shortly after, she had accepted David Frydman's offer to join Ariès.

She bent over the desk and examined Mayoux's report. It had been word-processed on a computer and printed by a serial printer. "Wait," the young woman suddenly said. "I know this printer."

The brothers looked at her in surprise. How could anybody recognize the typeface of a printer? After all, there were thousands of them in Paris.

Morisse went into the adjoining office and came back a few minutes later, holding a letter. She showed the two brothers that the type in the two documents was identical. "They were both printed on a Macintosh printer," she said. "And that printer is the one used by Jean-Marie Degueldre, L'Oréal's lawyer." Then she added, "And I'll prove it!"

Morisse's allegations were extremely serious. If she was right, that meant that Mayoux had printed his "impartial" report in the offices of L'Oréal's lawyer.

Catherine Morisse would turn out to be right. An expert, Robert Fontaine, accredited by the Paris courts, studied the documents she submitted to him. On May 24, 1991, he would formally confirm that Mayoux's report had been printed in Degueldre's office. (The expert also had an offer for Catherine Morisse: If she ever needed a job, he would be delighted to employ her.)

The young woman didn't stop at that. She checked the postmark on the registered envelope in which Mayoux's report had been sent to the court, and made another discovery. The report had been sent from a post office situated near Degueldre's law firm—and very far from Mayoux's office. Besides providing the computer and printer, L'Oréal's representatives had possibly mailed Mayoux's report as well.

A final discovery concerned Charles Leguide. As Paravision's comptroller, he had been asked to prepare a detailed financial report on which Mayoux would base his conclusions. It transpired that on June 27, 1990, Mayoux had called Leguide and demanded his report right away. Leguide had protested, saying the report wasn't completed yet, but Mayoux wouldn't listen. He finally forced Leguide to deliver his incomplete report at 6 P.M.

The sequence of events was now clear: On June 25, Jobert and Frydman had discovered Mayoux's links with L'Oréal. Mayoux had rejected their demand to resign the following day. But worried by the exposure of his L'Oréal connection, he had hurriedly completed his report, had it typed in the office of L'Oréal's lawyer, and mailed it to the court in advance. He then calmly told the court that his association with L'Oréal had ended in 1988, whereas in truth he had continued working as a consultant for the company until the end of 1989.

The Frydman brothers appealed the findings of Mayoux's report and accused him of fraud.

In the trial that followed, Mayoux's lawyers would admit that his report had indeed been typed and printed in the offices of Jean-Marie Degueldre. This had been done, they said, because it was late in the evening and

Mayoux had no secretary. Frydman's new attorney, Maître Bernard Jouanneau, ridiculed this answer. "Mr. Mayoux has his own office and secretary at the Société
Générale," he said. "Hasn't he ever heard of overtime
work for extra pay? Besides, he got 1.2 million francs
[about $220,000] for his work. Couldn't he hire a secre-
tary for a few hours?"

On April 9, 1992, the Paris Court of Appeals annulled
Mayoux's report.

On December 9, 1992, the Paris District Court found
Jacques Mayoux guilty of fraud and ordered him to re-
imburse the fee of 600,000 francs he had been paid by
the Frydman brothers.

On May 12, 1995, the Paris Court of Appeals sat to
hear the appeal of Jacques Mayoux. He and L'Oréal were
represented by two celebrated lawyers, the *bâtonniers* (bar
association presidents) Bondoux and Grandrut. They tried
to undermine the credibility of the Frydman brothers,
maintaining they were motivated by greed. Maître Bernard
Jouanneau, Frydman's lawyer, pleaded brilliantly, refuting
their arguments one after the other.

On June 30, 1995, the Court of Appeals delivered its
decision. The court not only confirmed the 1992 verdict
but augmented the fraud judgment against Jacques Mayoux. L'Oréal and Mayoux were ordered to pay the costs
of the trial. A new expert would be appointed to determine
the value of the Frydmans' portion of Paravision.

Five years—to the day—had passed since that figure
was originally supposed to be established. As so often
with the legal system, justice was slow in coming.

But meanwhile, on other fronts, things were hap-
pening.

6

On February 22, 1991, at 9:30 P.M., the warhead of a SCUD missile launched from a mobile pad in western Iraq hit Savyon, a Tel Aviv suburb of lush gardens and sprawling villas. The warhead destroyed a house on Hatichon Street, killing a man and his dog, then slid across the street, slammed through the front of Jean Frydman's home, and exploded in his living room. Luckily, Frydman's house was unoccupied. The previous evening he had flown to Paris.

He had spent most of the Gulf War in Israel. Had he stayed another day in Savyon, he too would have been a victim of the SCUD's direct hit.

Back in Paris, Frydman was waging his private war against L'Oréal. Several months before, he had acted just as he had said he would before the Mayoux arbitration. On December 17, 1990, with the financial settlement temporarily put on hold, he had gone to the Palais de Justice, situated on the majestic Ile de la Cité which bisects the river Seine. There he had pressed charges against L'Oréal for perjury, use of falsified commercial documents, and racial discrimination in an economic activity. He had chosen as his lawyer Bernard Jouanneau.

Erect, stocky, and bald, an intellectual and an art lover, Jouanneau specialized in the laws governing artistic and musical property. A man of great moral probity, he had joined the Ligue Contre le Racisme et l'Antisemitisme—the League Against Racism and Anti-Semitism—in 1972 and was elected its vice president. Though he wasn't Jewish, he had become one of the most passionate fighters against Holocaust deniers such as the notorious professor Faurisson. He studied the history of the Holocaust and traveled to Poland and to Israel, where he interviewed death camp survivors. He used their testimonies and the documents he researched to publicly refute Faurisson's assertions that the Holocaust hadn't happened.

"This is a lonely combat," Jouanneau once said. "It demands a vast historical research. It has changed my life."

With the same dedication he supported the struggle of the Armenians to make known the truth about their people's genocide. "Whenever there was an ideological combat, I was there." This outwardly calm fifty-year-old Parisian with a frank, unwavering gaze also struggled against the French right-wing extremist Jean-Marie Le Pen, whose racist views he abhorred. "The fact that I was not Jewish gave me the authority and the capacity for anger that Jewish lawyers didn't have."

His integrity was tested early in the L'Oréal affair. One of his best clients was Publicis, the leading advertising agency in France, which represented L'Oréal. Soon after he had agreed to take the Frydman brothers' case, he was discreetly warned by a Publicis executive that he shouldn't get involved in the L'Oréal affair if he wanted to retain Publicis as a client. A lesser man would have bent to this pressure, but Jouanneau was a rock of decency in the stormy waters of legal maneuvering. He believed in the Frydmans and wholeheartedly devoted himself to their defense. Soon after, he lost the Publicis contract.

Another model of probity emerged in the case, with far-reaching consequences.

In the French legal system, any new case is assigned to a *juge d'instruction*. This "judge" is a sort of district attorney who is responsible for gathering evidence and ruling whether the case is fit for trial. If the *juge d'instruction* concludes that the charges have merit, the case is handed to a court judge, who presides over the trial. A *juge d'instruction* cannot preside over a trial, nor can a court judge investigate a case. The Frydmans' chances of success in their case against L'Oréal depended heavily on what sort of *juge d'instruction* they got. Enter Judge Jean-Pierre Getti.

At the age of forty-seven, Getti had the reputation of a born fighter, a man of great integrity, tenacity, and courage. Short, wiry, with dark hair, bright eyes nestled under thick eyebrows, and a determined chin, Getti was a Parisian by birth, a cinema buff, and an avid reader. He had studied at the Faculty of Law in Paris, then at the School for Magistrates. A veteran of fifteen years, he was considered one of the most competent in his field. The Palais de Justice often assigned the most difficult cases to Judge Getti.

Over the years he had investigated many cases concerning crimes committed by his pro-Nazi countrymen in wartime France. Some of these became *causes célèbres*.

One of them was the Touvier investigation, which shook the entire country. Paul Touvier had been the Lyon

chief of the pro-Nazi Milice during the German occupation, and was responsible for a long string of murders. His
most odious crimes were the killings of seven Jews at
Rillieux-la-Pape and the assassination of Victor Brasch,
former president of the League of Human Rights, and his
wife, Hélène, both in their eighties. Twice sentenced to
death in absentia at the end of the war, Touvier was arrested several times but managed to escape and, with the
help of the Church lived in France for many years undis-
turbed. He had become a member of the fundamentalist
Confrérie des Chevaliers de Notre Dame—the Brother-
hood of the Knights of Our Lady—whose members protected him and hid him in several convents affiliated with
their organization.

After several *juges d'instruction* had failed to find
grounds for prosecution, or had given in to pressure, the
investigation of his case was entrusted to Judge Getti, who
finally brought Touvier to the bar of justice. Touvier's
victims were represented by the son of Nazi hunter Serge
Klarsfeld, attorney Arno Klarsfeld, who pleaded for a life
sentence; that indeed was imposed.

Getti had also investigated the charges against Jean
Leguay, the notorious assistant to the Vichy police chief
in 1942–43. Among other crimes Leguay had been of utmost assistance to the Gestapo in rounding up the Jews
of Paris for deportation. He had also suggested that the
Nazis deport children and several categories of foreign
Jews that the Gestapo hadn't even intended to arrest. After
the war he made his career in the perfume business, eventually becoming a senior executive of Nina Ricci. In a
foreshadowing of events to come, he was elected secretary
general of the Parfumerie Française with the help of top
executives at L'Oréal. For a while his offices were located
in a building owned by L'Oréal.

Leguay's past, and particularly his part in the deportation of the Paris Jews, were publicly exposed in the mid-seventies. After Getti's investigation, Leguay was indicted for crimes against humanity in 1979, but died in his bed ten years later, still not brought to trial.

Judge Getti had investigated the charges against several German Nazis as well. One of them was Klaus Barbie, the sadistic SS-Obersturmführer who deported trainloads of Dutch Jews before coming to France. He continued his monstrous work in Lyon, becoming responsible for the murders of 4,342 Resistance members, including the legendary hero Jean Moulin. In an act of astounding cynicism, Barbie was rescued after the war by the U.S. Central Intelligence Agency, which intended to use his knowledge and his anti-Communist zeal in the Cold War against the Soviet Union. Barbie was one of several German officers who were recruited by the CIA, in full knowledge of their war crimes. Later, the CIA smuggled Barbie to South America. He was finally extradited to France in 1983 and sentenced to life. He died in prison in 1991.

Another criminal that Getti investigated but didn't succeed in bringing to trial was Alois Brünner. This was the same man who had virtually snatched Jean Frydman from the firing squad and sent him to Germany, where, in good German *Ordnung*, a Jew was supposed to be exterminated. With fanatical tenacity Brünner had dispatched the Jews of Greece, France, and Slovakia—the total nearing 130,000—to the death camps.

After the war Brünner escaped to Damascus, where he still lives in full freedom. Serge Klarsfeld and his brave wife, Beate, tried to get him arrested in Damascus, but instead the Syrian police arrested *them* and expelled them from the country.

The most dramatic case in which Getti had taken part is the Bousquet affair. René Bousquet, secretary general of the French police and Leguay's direct superior, was the man responsible for the arrest and deportation of 60,000 Jews on the Germans' orders. Appreciated by Himmler ("He is a valuable collaborator"), often consulted by Vichy prime minister Pierre Laval, Bousquet was arrested after the war and condemned to a mere five years of "national degradation," which didn't include even a day in jail. His sentence was immediately annulled because of his "resistant activities."

Bousquet even had the cheek to run for Parliament in 1958, but was defeated. He became a banker and a businessman. Then, in 1991, he was indicted again following charges by Serge Klarsfeld. Klarsfeld created a national scandal by revealing that Bousquet was a close friend and political supporter of President Mitterrand, who knew all about his past. Judge Getti painstakingly prepared the evidence for the court, but Bousquet's trial never took place. On June 8, 1993, a mentally ill gunman ambushed the former Vichy police chief and shot him dead.

So this was the fiber of the man who, in December 1990, was entrusted with the Frydman file. Judge Getti's task was to establish whether or not the charges pressed by Frydman against L'Oréal had a solid basis. This required first a thorough study of the boycott issue.

He learned that the Arab boycott had started as early as December 2, 1945. Two and a half years before the State of Israel was born, the Arab League council had adopted Resolution 16, which stated that the Arab nations would boycott "Jewish products and manufactured goods." The boycott was reinforced by Resolution 70 in 1946. Finally, after the creation of Israel in 1948, the Arab

League established the Boycott Bureau, a mammoth organization based in Damascus.

The boycott was applied on several levels. The "primary" boycott was a solemn commitment by the Arab states not to purchase any Israeli products. The "secondary" boycott was against non-Arab companies that traded with Israel. The "tertiary" boycott targeted companies that did business with companies violating the boycott rules. Finally, there was the "personal" boycott, which blacklisted people, companies, and organizations known to be pro-Zionist or pro-Israeli.

The boycott blatantly violated international law, as well as flouting the principles of free trade. Several western nations reacted with tough antiboycott legislation. In the United States, a law was passed at the federal level, known as 50 U.S.C. § 2401. The State of New York passed N.Y. Exec. L. § 296(13). The United States also created an institution to fight the boycott: the Office of Anti-Boycott Compliance of the U.S. Department of Commerce.

For many years France didn't take action against the boycott, unwilling to irritate the Arab nations. She called herself a "Muslim power." Close ties bound her to her former colonies and protectorates in North Africa. Syria and Lebanon had also been under French rule until World War II, and France had interests in Egypt and other countries in the Middle East. These connections made France shape a pro-Arab policy, which also resulted in a reserved attitude toward Israel since its creation.

French policy changed in 1954, when armed rebellion erupted in Algeria, aimed at freeing the country from French rule. The rebels of the FLN—Front de Libération Nationale—were supported by many Arab nations, but most of all by Egypt's president, Gamal Abdel Nasser. He considered himself the leader of the Arab world, and had shaped a theory of Pan-Arabism, according to which all Arabs were to unite under his leadership. He regarded Algeria's war of liberation as a part of the awakening of the Arab world. He poured weapons into the FLN units and money into its coffers, and many FLN fighters were trained in Egypt. Under Nasser's leadership, many other Arab nations adopted a hostile attitude toward France and demanded that Algeria be given full independence.

France reacted by abandoning her traditional pro-Arab policy. Deciding to crush Nasser, she became a close ally of Israel. From 1954 to 1956, Nasser was arming Palestinian terrorists, the "Fedayeen," and dispatching them into Israel from bases in the Gaza Strip. The terrorists attacked civilian targets, spreading death and destruction. Israel retaliated by attacking Egyptian army bases. The border clashes often turned into full-scale battles, with the artillery and even the air forces joining the fray. France decided to arm Israel in view of a probable war with Egypt. At that time Israel was considering a preemptive war against Egypt, following a mammoth arms deal between Egypt and Czechoslovakia signed in the late summer of 1955. In this Soviet-inspired deal, Egypt was to receive more than a hundred jet fighters and bombers, hundreds of tanks and cannons, submarines, and other weapons.

War became inevitable when, in 1956, Egypt blocked Israeli shipping from entering the Red Sea; Nasser also angered the Western nations by nationalizing the Suez Canal. In October 1956, Israeli prime minister David Ben-Gurion secretly flew to Paris with the chief of staff of the Israeli army, General Moshe Dayan, and the director general of the defense ministry, Shimon Peres. He held talks with France's leaders and the British foreign minister, and signed a secret agreement that amounted to a military alliance.

On October 29, 1956, a few days after Ben-Gurion returned home, Israel launched its Sinai Campaign against Egypt. During that war France acted as Israel's close ally, supplying weapons and even sending air force and navy units to protect Israel's territory. Simultaneously, France joined forces with England, and their armies landed in Egypt in an attempt to gain control over the Suez Canal. After a few days of fighting, the French and British bowed to joint American and Soviet pressure, and pulled their forces from Egyptian soil. This fiasco, called "the last colonial war," poisoned their relations with the Arab world for years to come.

Israel, on the other hand, won its war, and the French-Israeli alliance continued for another ten years. France became the major weapons supplier to the Israeli army.

The Algerian war, however, ended in 1962, under de Gaulle's presidency. France pulled out of Algeria, which was granted full independence. The main obstacle to a reconciliation between France and the Arab world was thus removed, and France gradually moved back to her traditional positions. The moment of truth came in 1967, when Nasser blocked the Red Sea access again and threatened Israel with a war of destruction. On June 5, 1967, Israel launched the Six-Day War, defeating Egypt, Jordan, and Syria, and occupying the Sinai, the West Bank of the Jordan, Jerusalem, and the Golan Heights. This time, however, France was no longer Israel's ally. On the eve of the war President de Gaulle had decided to change sides, and imposed an arms embargo upon Israel.

After the Six-Day War, France became a pro-Arab nation again, and her relations with Israel turned cold, even strained. For fear of angering her Arab allies, France docilely yielded to the Arab boycott. Not until June 7, 1977, did two Gaullist members of parliament present an antiboycott bill before the National Assembly. It was approved, but six weeks after its passage, Prime Minister Raymond Barre published a decree that suspended the law's application in the Middle East. Barre feared that Arab countries might retaliate by reducing their trade with France. He therefore yielded to the very requirements of the Arab boycott that the law was designed to oppose.

In 1980 the Conseil d'État (justice department) annulled Barre's decree, but Barre changed the wording and published it again. The antiboycott law therefore remained suspended until the presidential elections of 1981. During the campaign François Mitterrand solemnly promised the president of the French Jewish community, Alain de Rothschild, that France would comply no longer with the boycott.

After Mitterrand won the election, he announced that he intended to implement the antiboycott law. Various members of his cabinet initially objected. Joining the foreign minister, Claude Cheysson, was Jacques Delors, the finance minister, and the minister for foreign trade, Michel Jobert. They feared a catastrophic decline in France's trade with the Arab world. "This law might cost us between two and three hundred thousand jobs," Delors warned.

Prime Minister Pierre Mauroy was adamant, however. In a meeting with the recalcitrant ministers, he stood up, his face purple with fury, and snapped: "You know what the president expects of you. I'm leaving now. When you've finished writing the new decree, reactivating the law, come back and see me!"

Two hours later, the decree was indeed ready, and on

July 19, 1981, it was officially enacted. Since that day, Articles 187-2 and 416-1 of the Penal Code, Laws 77-574 and 85-772, have prohibited economic discrimination against any person or company "because of their national origins, of their belonging or not belonging . . . to a certain nation, a race, or a religion." The penalty for violating the law is a prison sentence of two months to a year and a fine of 2,000 to 20,000 francs.

Getti's first impression was that, although unusual, Frydman's serious allegations seemed to be supported. That Frydman's attorney was Bernard Jouanneau also impressed him. "I didn't know Frydman," Getti later said, "but I knew Bernard Jouanneau, with whom I had worked on certain cases in the past. When Jouanneau accepts a case, it is always based on something solid and concrete. He would never embark upon an adventure without a certain number of assets in his pocket."

Nonetheless, Frydman was lucky that Judge Getti had been assigned to his case. Besides Getti's excellent record, he was also legendary for his independence. The tough, determined judge wouldn't yield to pressure of any kind, not even from the highest echelon.

And pressure from the top, Frydman now realized, was the danger he had to fear most. President Mitterrand was a close friend of François Dalle and of L'Oréal's owner, André Bettencourt. The power of L'Oréal and its political connections were good enough reasons for many French civil servants, and certainly for district attorneys and police officers, to refrain from touching the L'Oréal affair.

Besides, the affair was growing into a gigantic tangle that might occupy the French courts far into the twenty-first century. Shortly after the conflict between L'Oréal and Jean Frydman had started, L'Oréal had decided to counter his suit with a lawsuit of their own. The cosmetics company probably wanted to create an impression of "balance" as much as to seek compensation for real or imaginary grievances. The Frydman brothers countered L'Oréal's suit with another one; L'Oréal retaliated, and the cases multiplied like mushrooms.

An impartial observer might have pointed out that Frydman had no tangible evidence against L'Oréal. The corporation angrily denied it had surrendered to the Boycott Bureau's blackmail. In addition, Frydman accused Corrèze of having planned and overseen his eviction from Paravision, but he had nothing to support that allegation except for his side's account of a conversation with Michel Pietrini—who had meanwhile changed his version and now denied any implication of Corrèze. Finally, he accused Pietrini and Dalle of faking the minutes of a non-existent meeting of Paravision's board, but he had no papers to prove that either.

Judge Getti could have handled Frydman's complaint with kid gloves. After all, L'Oréal was a top-performing French company, bringing billions of francs in profits, taxes, and foreign currency into the national coffers. L'Oréal was also the embodiment of French notions of beauty and refinement. Burying the affair would be viewed sympathetically, even considered a patriotic gesture.

Most of Getti's colleagues would have called their superior and asked what to do with the case. The response probably would have been "informal advice" to refrain from showing an excess of zeal in the matter—in other words, don't conduct a real investigation.

But Getti wasn't that kind of man.

Knowing how politically loaded the Frydman-L'Oréal

affair was, he first had to make sure that the law enforcement officer working with him on the investigation
wouldn't yield to any political pressure. In France, all investigations are carried out by the Police Judiciaire, a
branch constituted of regular police units and gendarmerie
units. Getti decided not to appoint a regular police officer
to the case. Police officers are trained to ask for authorization from their superiors at every step of the way.

"Say a police officer is charged with investigating the
L'Oréal affair," a French official put it. "He would pick
up the phone and call his chief, who would call the assistant to the interior minister, who would call the minister
himself. And then the minister would say go ahead—or
don't go ahead."

Getti used a different approach, choosing the gendarmerie wing of the Police Judiciare instead. The gendarmerie is formally a part of the army, and no interior
or justice minister can tell a gendarmerie officer what to
do. Getti decided to appoint as his assistant a gendarmerie
officer with whom he had worked in the past, in the investigation of the Touvier and the Bousquet affairs: Colonel Jean-Louis Recordon.

Colonel Recordon was the chief of the gendarmerie's
investigation brigade in Paris. Slim, with short salt-and-
pepper hair, spectacles, and a neatly trimmed mustache,
he was a man of moral and intellectual principles. To his
friends he used to say that three great Frenchmen had
influenced his views on life when he still was a student;
later they had affected his job as investigator as well. The
first was the philosopher Descartes, whose iron-clad logical approach Recordon considered a basic element of his
French heritage. From the second, Montaigne, he had
adopted the principle of always maintaining the element
of doubt, "the first principle of the investigator." And

finally, Pascal had taught him that even acts of the highest authority, like God, shouldn't be accepted blindly, but only after being explained in full detail and on logical grounds.

Recordon had an impressive record. As a young soldier he had distinguished himself in the Algerian war. After graduating from the Gendarmerie Officers Academy and the Criminology Institute, he had been put in charge of the gendarmerie training school before joining the Police Judiciaire. Among his high-profile investigations was the dramatic case of the AIDS-contaminated blood, in which many members of the health-care establishment knowingly compromised the blood banks of France. The senior staff of the National Center of Blood Transfusion were well aware that heating their stocks of blood according to an American procedure would eliminate the AIDS virus—but they refrained, on the grounds that the process was expensive. As a result, many people throughout France contracted AIDS and hepatitis through transfusions, and hundreds—some say thousands—died. A number of prominent doctors were indicted, tried, and jailed, and several cabinet ministers, accused of criminal negligence, were still awaiting trial as of mid 1996.

Recordon had also been assigned to most of the cases of crimes against humanity. He had investigated the case of Alois Brünner. He had prepared the files on René Bousquet and worked on the Klaus Barbie trial. The case of which he was most proud was the investigation and arrest of Paul Touvier. He had worked on that case with Judge Getti, and the two men had a great deal of respect for each other. "I trusted him completely," Judge Getti said. "With him I knew that my rear was solid, and if I entrusted him with a mission, that mission would be well prepared and well executed."

One afternoon in January 1991, Recordon was working in his drab office at 12 rue de Béarn in the historic
Marais quarter. It was a squalid apartment building, with
family quarrels echoing in the halls, cooking smells drift-
ing out of open doors, rusty bicycles blocking the en-
trance, and children's soccer balls bouncing on the stairs.
The gendarmerie offices were cold and poorly equipped.
The officers couldn't even afford a computer for word-
processing their paperwork. Recordon's phone rang and
he found it was Judge Getti. "I think I have something
for you," the judge said.

Recordon hurried to the judge's office in the Palais de
Justice. Getti handed him Jean Frydman's file, and Recordon read the charges involving Israel, the Arab boycott,
and L'Oréal. He could see that this was a unique sort of
case. "Yes, I'm interested," he said to Getti. The judge
signed his appointment, then gave him Frydman's statement. "Study this thing and call me," he said.

At that time Recordon was in charge of forty officers
working on a hundred criminal files in different stages of
investigation. Still, the Frydman file intrigued him, and he
took it home to read that night.

The following morning, he sent several of his men to
the Tribunal de Commerce to get the files on Paravision
and L'Oréal and instructed others to prepare a written history of L'Oréal and Cosmair. He then conferred with
Judge Getti, and the two men agreed on a strategy. First
they had to find out if Frydman's accusations would bear
scrutiny. For this they had to check out several crucial
points in his deposition. Although it was obvious that they
eventually had to interview Jean Frydman, they preferred
as their first witness his brother, David, whose testimony
could corroborate, or weaken, Jean's version of the events.

On March 7, 1991, David Frydman was summoned to

Recordon's office. He was sworn, then testified for thirteen hours over two days, describing his brother's life, his exploits in the Resistance, his career in radio and television, the creation of Paravision, the strategic committee meeting, the false letter of resignation.

Recordon found the story both deeply moving and intriguing. When David Frydman described the connections of L'Oréal with La Cagoule, and mentioned the name of Corrèze, Recordon was electrified. He had always been a history buff. One of his great delights was to open an old file, full of yellow-edged documents, and find himself transported to some dramatic chapter in his country's past. The war years in particular fascinated him.

He didn't show his feelings, though. When David Frydman's testimony was finished, he politely sent him home. Turning to his deputy, Adjutant Philippe Mathy, he asked him to find out everything he could about Jacques Corrèze. Then he met with Judge Getti.

"What do you think?" the judge said. "Solid? Not solid?"

"This is an interesting affair," Recordon said. In their private vocabulary this meant that David Frydman was a credible witness.

That was the moment when the entire investigation might have been aborted. If Recordon hadn't been favorably impressed by David Frydman's testimony, he would have said so to Getti and the judge could have closed the file. But on the basis of his deposition, they decided to bring in Jean Frydman. This time Getti himself was on hand to hear the testimony.

Jean Frydman introduced a wealth of new elements, mostly about Corrèze and Cosmair, the huge American sister company of L'Oréal that belonged to Corrèze, Dalle, and Bettencourt. Corrèze was in Paris now, living in a splendid apartment overlooking the Seine.

Corrèze, added Frydman, was not the only former Nazi who had worked at L'Oréal. Through their research the Frydman brothers had discovered that at the end of the war, several fugitives had found a refuge in L'Oréal. Their trails all passed through Spain. The first to arrive, in 1945, were Henri Deloncle, the brother of La Cagoule's founder Eugène Deloncle, and Eugène's twenty-one-year-old son, Louis.

In 1947 the American intelligence services reported from Madrid that a clandestine organization had been formed in Spain calling itself "88" or Dos Ochos. The name was a kind of secret password. Dos Ochos—two eights—sounded like "*dos hachas*"—two H's—which stood for *Heil Hitler*. The "88" members included German Nazis who had belonged to the Gestapo and the *Sicherheitsdienst* (SD), and Frenchmen who had belonged to the French Gestapo, the Legion of French Volunteers, and the Milice. The American report stressed that Henri Deloncle was a prominent member of Dos Ochos.

By this time Deloncle worked for the Spanish branch of L'Oréal, and so did his nephew, Louis. When L'Oréal created a new subsidiary, Procasa, Henri and Louis Deloncle worked there with one of the founders and a major shareholder of the company, whom they had known years ago—Jacques Corrèze.

Forty years later, Louis Deloncle had become the president of Procasa.

Another former Nazi and member of La Cagoule, Jean Azéma, had been a member of the Milice general staff. He had been an anchorman at the collaborationist Radio France and had served in the Waffen SS. After the war he too worked for Procasa before emigrating to Argentina, where he landed a position at Yuste, an advertising agency that handled L'Oréal. According to *Libération* reporter Annette Lévy-Willard, Yuste had been bought by the French publicity group Havas at L'Oréal's request. Inside Yuste, Jean Azéma was considered "L'Oréal's man." When the company's advertising account was transferred to another agency, Azéma went with it.

Jean Lévy, a former vice president of Cosmair who traveled in Latin America for the company, met Azéma in Argentina. Azéma's nominal employment, Lévy was told, was fictitious. The Argentinean ad agency that paid Azéma belonged to Havas, and Havas was paid by L'Oréal, keeping the payment by L'Oréal to Azéma indirect.

Swinging through Mexico on this same trip, Jean Lévy found another former member of the Mouvement Social Révolutionnaire and the Milice who was employed by L'Oréal—Jacques Piquet, who worked for L'Oréal's computer services. On his return, Lévy went to François Dalle and told him about the two criminals who worked for his company. "You're a muckraker!" Dalle allegedly answered.

In addition, the Frydman brothers claimed that L'Oréal had employed war criminals Jean-Pierre Ingrand, Guy Servant, and Gabriel Jeantet, but they could not substantiate their accusations with documents. Ingrand had been one of Bousquet's assistants. Servant had joined the LVF, besides being implicated in the murder of Maurice Sarraut, an enemy of Laval, in Toulouse. Jeantet had been a deputy of Deloncle in La Cagoule.

According to the Frydman brothers, L'Oréal had also offered a job to Michel Harispe, another La Cagoule member, who was condemned to death by a French court for murders carried out during the war, and who at a certain period had served directly under Corrèze. L'Oréal denied the allegation, stating that Harispe had died in prison after the war. It admitted, though, that Harispe's son worked for the company as a driver.

The gravest accusation by Jean and David Frydman concerned Jean Filliol, the bloodiest criminal La Cagoule had produced. Nobody knows how many people he killed with his own hands, but some historians have advanced the number of a hundred. He has also been accused of a most appalling crime. In June 1944, when Filliol served as head of intelligence for the Milice in Limoges, he was asked by the commanders of the SS Division Das Reich for information on the whereabouts of one of their officers, captured by the Resistance. Filliol steered the revenge-thirsty SS to a village called Oradour-sur-Glane. There the Nazis engaged in an orgy of killing, mowing down the men with machine guns and burning the old, the women, and the children in the church where they had taken refuge. Six hundred and forty people died in Oradour on June 10, 1944.

Jean Filliol, the Frydman brothers claimed, had escaped to Spain as well. Using his son's adopted name, André Lamy, he worked for many years at Procasa. (He later vanished and may still be alive.) L'Oréal angrily denied those charges as well, admitting, though, that André Lamy worked for many years for Procasa, and for L'Oréal in France.

Even if all of the Frydman brothers' charges couldn't be substantiated, it seemed clear that L'Oréal had employed not only Corrèze, Piquet, and Azéma but also the sons of La Cagoule's most notorious killers.

For Jean Frydman this was proof that there had been a clear pattern in L'Oréal's behavior after the war. It had systematically provided shelter to war criminals who shared a common bond—they all had been friends of Eugène Schueller, L'Oréal's founder and La Cagoule's enthusiastic sponsor.

For Judge Getti, however, the employment of former Nazis by L'Oréal was not germane to the case at hand. He had only to establish whether the cosmetics company had broken the law and yielded to the Arab boycott. Even so, because of its dark past, the L'Oréal affair had ominous political overtones.

Getti and Recordon met again after Jean Frydman's testimony.

"Careful," Getti said, "this is very delicate. François Dalle isn't a nobody."

Both of them knew they were embarking upon perilous waters.

Getti was determined to go ahead, but he had to determine how. He feared that if he summoned the heads of L'Oréal to his office, all possible evidence still kept in the company archives would disappear. "If I called Dalle and discussed the affair with him, the case was lost," he said later. "I had to go straight to the core of the matter, and put my hands on the documents. Once I got the papers, I could demand explanations from both sides. But without written evidence the case was dead."

"We must move quickly," Recordon said. "We can't keep the affair secret for long now."

"So what do you suggest?"

"A raid," Recordon said. "Raids on Paravision, L'Oréal, and the private homes of everybody involved." Only by launching a series of surprise raids could they seize the documents concerning the boycott and Frydman's phony resignation. "Raids at several places," he went on, "the same day, the same time. A simultaneous operation. Early in the morning."

The plan involved a tremendous risk. Raiding the offices of a prestigious French firm, bursting into the apartments of respectable tycoons—such a thing had never been done before. It was the height of insolence, and the gendarmerie officer was laying his career on the line— perhaps the judge's as well. Besides, two years had passed since the affair had taken place. The files probably had been purged in the meantime. If they came out of the Centre Eugène Schueller empty-handed, Getti and Recordon would have a lot of explaining to do.

That's why, when Recordon suggested a surprise raid, Judge Getti could have said, "Let me think it over," or "Come to see me again tomorrow, we'll discuss that." It would have been the end of the affair.

But the *juge d'instruction* cast a mischievous look at the colonel. "This will make some noise," he said with the shadow of a smile. "Don't you think?"

7

A t six o'clock on March 28, 1991, Colonel Recordon put on his uniform and phoned his assistants. He checked that all of the forty gendarmes who had been designated for the day's operation were ready. Then he gave the order. Six teams fanned out through Paris, heading for the headquarters of Paravision and L'Oréal, for the Clavier law offices, and for the homes of Michel Pietrini, Mare Ladreit de Lacharrière, and Jacques Corrèze. In a second stage they would raid several other offices and private homes of L'Oréal executives.

Judge Getti too made a phone call, to inform his superiors of the impending raid. He had deliberately waited until a half hour before the raid started.

"It was clear to me," he later said, "that with a company like L'Oréal, which was extremely powerful, extremely well organized, with a very competent legal department, I couldn't afford to let a piece of evidence disappear. A raid at dawn, with uniformed gendarmes, isn't undertaken lightly. The method we used was brutal,

I concede, but very efficient. My tactic was to not warn anybody beforehand. If I wanted to seize the important documents before they disappeared, I had to keep the utmost secrecy."

Getti was also alive to the possibility of intervention, disguised as "friendly" advice, by a top official—another reason to keep silent until the last moment.

Recordon personally headed for the apartment of François Dalle on Avenue Frédéric-Le Play, near the Eiffel Tower. But he soon realized he had made a mistake. Dalle didn't live at the apartment anymore, only his estranged wife, Geneviève. Dalle had moved to the Boulevard d'Argenson in the posh suburb of Neuilly. Recordon sent a team to Dalle's address with instructions to wait outside and prevent Dalle from leaving the house. Then he hurried back to his car and drove across Paris.

By now it was 8:30, the height of the morning rush hour, and the streets were clogged. Recordon turned on his police siren and sped forward, stopping traffic, climbing onto sidewalks, darting down one-way streets. It was hair-raising, but he finally rang at Dalle's door.

François Dalle was shocked and indignant to see several gendarmerie officers at his door. A police raid early in the morning is a humiliating experience, especially for one of France's most powerful and respected businessmen. Recordon and his men searched the house, even Dalle's briefcase. Dalle's staff—butler, driver, gardener, bodyguard—watched in silence. When he realized the raid had resulted from Jean Frydman's complaint, the elderly gentleman became even angrier. He showed Recordon the ribbon of the Légion d'Honneur, the highest French decoration, that he wore in his lapel. "Do you know what this is?" he asked.

"Yes, sir, absolutely."

"I am a former Resistance member."

"I know."

"Do you know who my friends are?" he said, possibly hinting at President Mitterrand.

"Yes, I do," Recordon answered. "But you also are a citizen from whom the law has the right to demand explanations. I don't know if you are guilty or innocent. I respect you as a citizen, and it is true that you bear one of the highest decorations of the Republic, that you have been a great resistant. You also are a business leader, and I respect you for all that. But I have to fulfill my duty."

The search at Dalle's house didn't produce any evidence, however, and Recordon asked Dalle to accompany him to L'Oréal headquarters. Dalle looked at Recordon's small automobile and asked, "Why don't you join me in my car?" He apparently didn't want to be driven to L'Oréal in a police car.

Recordon acceded and the two men left in Dalle's chauffeur-driven car. While they drove, Dalle couldn't stop attacking the Frydman brothers. They are scoundrels, he said, they are nothing. He, on the other hand, belonged to a major company, enjoyed a lot of support, had influential friends. Recordon sympathized with the old man. But he kept repeating that the charges must be investigated.

At L'Oréal, twelve of Recordon's gendarmes were waiting, visibly upset. When they had arrived earlier, the L'Oréal private guards had refused to let them in, then insisted that they leave their guns outside. In response, the gendarmes had pulled their weapons and lined the guards against the wall. The guards' behavior improved miraculously. They still looked stunned, though. There had never been a police raid on L'Oréal. It was simply inconceivable.

Recordon telephoned Judge Getti. "I am at Mr. Dalle's office," he said. "You can come, Judge." A half hour later, when Judge Getti arrived, Recordon was extremely tense. He quietly told Getti, "I'm going to look for evidence that the board meeting of March 30, 1989, didn't take place. If we don't find this, we are in big trouble, and Frydman has lost his case."

He left the two men in the office and stepped outside. His men had collected Dalle's appointment books for the last few years, and Recordon picked up the one for 1989. He turned the pages until he reached March 30.

One look was enough to realize they had hit the jackpot. On March 30 Dalle had been out of the country; he couldn't have attended any board meeting. But the official minutes of the meeting specified Dalle had been present when Frydman had handed in his resignation letter. The minutes, therefore, were completely phony.

At that moment one of Recordon's gendarmes rushed into the outer office. "Look what I found, boss," he said. He gave him a small book, edited by the Arab League, detailing the boycott rules. It contained different sections covering various economic activities. The gendarme also had some letters exchanged between L'Oréal and the Arab boycott offices.

Recordon, immensely relieved, approached the judge. "We've got them," he said. "On March 30, Dalle was not in Paris. We also have papers on the boycott. We've won."

Several hours later the gendarmes left L'Oréal, carrying almost half a ton of documents.

Getti and Recordon had long since departed to visit the other locations of the raid. Recordon drove to the Clavier law firm, which had established the legal report about the March 30 board meeting. From the information he had gathered, he already was familiar with the current practice in the dealings of Clavier with Paravision. Catherine Morisse, Paravision's legal counsel, would call Clavier's people and inform them of a board meeting, its date, and its subject, and they would make up the official documents registering the meeting.

When Recordon reached the Clavier offices, eight gendarmes were waiting uncertainly. Furious, the senior partner had refused to let them search the premises. After all, Clavier was one of the most prominent law firms in Paris. Recordon calmly ordered everybody to leave except for the top executives, who were confined to their rooms. "We are calling the shots now," he said.

The gendarmes blocked the phone lines. As the senior partner kept protesting, Recordon said, "Listen, you're going to stay here as long as I say. I'll send away whoever I want, I'll arrest whoever I want."

"Who do you think you are?" the lawyer fired back. "Do you know who François Dalle is?"

"Don't worry about him," Recordon answered. "He's already in custody."

The man grew pale and slumped into his chair.

The gendarmes quickly found what they were looking for: the records and notes concerning the Paravision board meetings. They departed with a heavy load.

Other places raided that morning were Paravision's offices on the Champs-Élysées, the former L'Oréal headquarters on rue Royale, and the private homes of "O.J." and several L'Oréal and Paravision executives.

In a beautiful apartment overlooking the Seine, Recordon's gendarmes found Jacques Corrèze. He was an old man, almost bald, with waxen skin. When the gendarmes read the search orders, he reacted angrily. "This investigation of yours, it's bullshit," he muttered. "Do you know who I am? Do you know I am a relative of your boss? Yes, President Mitterrand. I am a relative of François Mitterrand."

The arrogant executive reluctantly answered a few questions. He said he had no professional activities in France, where he was staying temporarily. He worked for L'Oréal, in the field of international trade, and was chairman of Cosmair in the United States. He carried a French and a Spanish passport, for he had lived in Spain for a few years after 1950.

He was tough and confident. "I don't regret anything I did in my life," he added with a shrug. "You can search the house, I don't care. I am very sick, I've got terminal cancer, I'm going to die. It's a question of a few weeks. Do whatever you want."

8

"The fishing was good," Judge Getti cautiously said to Bernard Jouanneau, the Frydmans' lawyer, a week later. "But I won't let anybody come close to the documents for a long time."

The top executives of L'Oréal were in a state of shock. The police had never before raided their premises, never entered their homes and searched their briefcases. The experience was a humiliation for one of the finest French companies and for its bosses. It was also a sharp challenge to François Dalle and André Bettencourt, personal friends of the president.

By his dramatic move, however, Getti had obtained what he was looking for. In fact, the evidence unearthed exceeded his wildest expectations.

In his office at the Palais de Justice, the judge and his assistants sifted through thousands of documents from L'Oréal's files. The judge couldn't believe his eyes. Not only had L'Oréal's top executives lied when they solemnly declared they hadn't yielded to the Arab boycott, but they had also imprudently preserved their full correspondence with the boycott authorities. The raid on L'Oréal had produced a rich harvest of secret documents that told an ugly story of concealment, blackmail, and bribery.

In 1983 L'Oréal had discreetly started to acquire the Helena Rubinstein group of companies. The operation had been carried out mostly through Cosmair, since Jacques Corrèze had been a close acquaintance of the company founder. Once Madame Rubinstein was dead, her heirs were willing to sell the company and all its subsidiaries throughout the world. The company was sold first to Colgate Palmolive in 1973, and then, after another change of ownership in 1980, it was finally sold to L'Oréal in 1984. L'Oréal also started buying the international subsidiaries of Helena Rubinstein, but the Israeli subsidiary was then spun off to a local group, Ossem Ltd.

The acquisition of Helena Rubinstein by L'Oréal was completed in 1988. For that purpose L'Oréal used two front companies, the Switzerland-based SCIP and the Panama-based Palac.

Once Corrèze had bought all of the company's shares, he merged it with Cosmair and became Helena Rubinstein's chairman. But he soon found out that the company was blacklisted by the Arab Boycott Bureau, both because of Madame Rubinstein's Zionist views and because of the existence of a Helena Rubinstein plant in Israel.

In May 1984 came the first inquiry from the boycott bureau branch in Kuwait. L'Oréal, apparently trying to stall, replied in a declaration of May 28 that it was "completely independent of the Helena Rubinstein group" and had no relations with it. (Two years later the same official who signed the declaration, Pierre Castres Saint-Martin, apologized to the boycott authorities for this declaration.)

The Boycott Bureau wasn't satisfied, and in March 1985 it sent a questionnaire to L'Oréal inquiring about the acquisition of Helena Rubinstein. In December, L'Oréal replied that "the principles and regulations of the boycott were not applicable to [L'Oréal]."

Another letter, however, arrived at L'Oréal's headquarters from Damascus, dated May 21, 1986, and signed by Mohammed el-Ajami, the director of the bureau. Strangely enough, the regional boycott bureau had become a part of the Syrian ministry of defense, and the letter bore its official logo and seal. It had been routed through Dr. Mustafa el-Sayed, L'Oréal's lawyer in Syria. The letter stated:

> L'Oréal has purchased, itself and through some of its subsidiaries, a number of companies belonging to Helena Rubinstein Co. Ltd., with whom it is forbidden to deal. . . . L'Oréal also purchased a great deal of commercial brands belonging to these companies, which are registered only in certain countries. . . . Moreover, the names of the companies purchased . . . and certain commercial brands are still bearing the trade name of Helena Rubinstein Co.
>
> In order to allow the Arab boycott offices to decide . . . about the behavior of L'Oréal, the company has to provide the following documents:
>
> 1. A complete set of copies of the contracts by which the company L'Oréal or its subsidiaries have purchased companies or commercial brands belonging to the American company Helena Rubinstein or any company belonging to it.
>
> 2. Bank documents proving the payment of the acquisition price . . . for any of the said companies.
>
> 3. The list of the names of the last directors of each

company of the group Helena Rubinstein before it was bought by L'Oréal, as well as the list of the names of their present directors.

4. A declaration by L'Oréal as well as its subsidiaries, its parent company Gesparal, and its subsidiaries, about its current relationship with the American company Helena Rubinstein Ltd. and the companies owned by it.

This declaration had to provide detailed answers about Helena Rubinstein's capital, industry authorizations, use of commercial brands, know-how, and representation on the boards of directors. Ajami also demanded "official documents from the trade register of the country where they are registered proving the change of name of the companies purchased by L'Oréal and the fact that the expression *Helena Rubinstein* or any other expression or name belonging to Helena Rubinstein is no more in use." Another paragraph in this letter of ultimatum required L'Oréal to supply the Boycott Bureau with "official documents" proving:

Either the withdrawal by L'Oréal and its subsidiaries of the totality of the commercial brands purchased from the Helena Rubinstein group—

Or the purchase by L'Oréal of the rights to these commercial brands worldwide, so that the Helena Rubinstein companies will no longer own and will not have any rights in the said brands in any country of the world.

In any case, the commercial brands in which the name Helena Rubinstein or its derivatives figure must be discontinued by the companies belonging to L'Oréal.

Ajami apparently was determined to wipe the name of Helena Rubinstein from the face of the earth. With fanatical attention to detail, he didn't leave any loophole in his demands. He asked "written proof for [a previous L'Oréal declaration] that the company does not participate in the capitals of other companies . . . and a list of the names and nationalities of all companies in which L'Oréal and its subsidiaries participate."

The letter went on to demand that L'Oréal and its parent company, Gesparal, supply "a new declaration describing truly the relationship with Israel with regard to the rules of the boycott." For that purpose the following questions were to be answered:

> Do you presently own, or have you owned in the past, a company or a plant, secondary or principal, or an assembling facility in Israel?
>
> Do you or did you ever have agencies or main offices in Israel for your affairs in the Middle East or your international affairs?
>
> Have you ever granted the right to use your name or any of your subsidiaries' names, commercial brands, patents . . . to Israeli citizens or organizations?
>
> Do you participate, or did you in the past participate, and do you or did you in the past own shares, in Israeli organizations or corporations either in Israel or out of Israel?
>
> Do you, or have you ever, provided counsel or technical assistance to any Israeli organization or enterprise?
>
> Are you presently a representative, or have you ever been one, of any Israeli organization or corporation?

These questions, and many others concerning Gesparal's and L'Oréal's structure and ownership, concluded Ajami's letter. L'Oréal was required to produce all the documents in two certified originals and twenty-five copies with translation into Arabic. The certifying had to be done by an Arab embassy in France, excluding the diplomatic missions of Egypt, which had signed a peace agreement with Israel.

This questionnaire was illegal under international as well as French law. But L'Oréal's officials didn't ignore it or complain to the French government. Quite the opposite. L'Oréal's financial and legal director, Pierre Castres Saint-Martin, wrote a declaration on October 3, 1986, in which he partially answered the Boycott Bureau's questions.

> We, L'Oréal, a French limited corporation . . . make the following statement in our own name . . . and in the name of the company Gesparal:
>
> We do not have . . . and did not have . . . a company or any activity in Israel.
>
> We do not and did not have any branch office or main office in Israel.
>
> We have not granted the right to use our name, commercial brands, patents of our inventions to Israeli persons or organizations.
>
> We have no participation in Israeli companies . . . are not giving technical assistance to Israeli companies . . . do not represent Israeli companies.

To that declaration Castres added a full list of L'Oréal's French and foreign subsidiaries, and had his signature witnessed and certified—at the French foreign ministry!

Castres Saint-Martin, an elegant, slim man with wire-rimmed glasses and a cleft chin, was the very image of a meticulous, efficient executive. A month later, on November 17, 1986, he sent to Syria another batch of documents, answering the boycott's requirements about various Helena Rubinstein subsidiaries around the world (Argentina, Brazil, Venezuela, Peru, Japan), proving that the companies had been dissolved or changed their names, and the directors everywhere had been replaced.

There was no doubt that L'Oréal had bent over backward in order to satisfy the Arab boycott demands. In the accompanying letter Castres stressed: "Our company, its subsidiaries, and its parent company have no relations with Israel, according to the rules and provisions of the boycott. L'Oréal has complied with all the regulations of the boycott of Israel."

That letter—again certified by the helpful foreign ministry of France, which was supposed to enforce its government's antiboycott laws—was dispatched to the defense ministry in Damascus.

In his letter Castres made one omission: the existing Helena Rubinstein plant in Israel. L'Oréal's top executives didn't know how to terminate Helena Rubinstein Israel, which didn't belong to them. HR Israel was an independent company, owned by Israeli businessmen. Therefore the L'Oréal bosses apparently chose to keep quiet and hope for the best.

They should have known better. The Arab League wanted the obliteration of the late Madame Rubinstein's company to be total. For its omission L'Oréal was going to pay a heavy price.

————

Throughout 1987 the boycott bureau and L'Oréal exchanged letters about several points on which L'Oréal's
answers hadn't satisfied the Damascus officials. Castres
Saint-Martin and his colleague Gérard Sanchez, from the
international legal department, repeatedly promised to
comply with the bureau requests and asked for an extension of the grace period accorded by the Arab League. In
the meantime, L'Oréal's officials were looking for other
means to escape the boycott.

Jacques Corrèze presented to his colleagues a project
called Opération Rocher. It was a rather far-fetched plan
to create a bogus company in Switzerland, with no apparent connections whatever with L'Oréal, that would buy
the Helena Rubinstein international operation.

Other L'Oréal officials thought that bribery might
solve the problem.

The idea was discussed in absolute secrecy, and
L'Oréal executives were careful not to have any documents
mentioning it typed up by a secretary. The intermediary
chosen for the negotiation with the Arabs was Abdallah
Abdel Bari, L'Oréal's representative in Cairo, a former director of *Al Ahram* newspaper and a friend of the late
president Sadat. In the secret documents exchanged by
L'Oréal's officials he was given the code name A/A.

The top-secret memos concerning him were handwritten. In a note sent by Gérard Sanchez to Castres Saint-
Martin on November 4, 1987, the money transfers were
discussed in veiled hints. The note was entitled "Negotiations with Damascus." It was apparently agreed that
L'Oréal would provide to the boycott bureau a portion of
the documents it had requested. An unspecified bank
would then send Abdel Bari a letter that had been drafted
by L'Oréal according to his instructions. Then the bribes
would be paid in two stages.

But the bribe system that had worked in the past, as far as L'Oréal's products in Israel were concerned, and that had kept the boycott bureau from acting on the Helena Rubinstein file since 1984, couldn't last forever. Though Abdel Bari enlisted the help of several middlemen in the Arab world, his efforts to get L'Oréal cleared in exchange for fat payoffs backfired. Finally, on March 22, 1988, the Arab Boycott Bureau decided to act.

A registered letter from Damascus arrived at L'Oréal headquarters in Clichy. It contained "Decree of Boycott no. 382," officially announcing that all Arab countries were banning all dealings with L'Oréal, Gesparal, and their fifty-five subsidiaries, including the perfumes Lancôme, Courrèges, and Guy Laroche.

L'Oréal's top executives were stunned. The banning of L'Oréal's products themselves was not so worrying. François Dalle had said cynically that the entire Arab market consumed barely the equivalent of a single French *département* in L'Oréal products. The danger was that the Arab boycott would keep spreading and infect L'Oréal's sister companies, the same way the ban on Helena Rubinstein had contaminated L'Oréal.

The next target of the Arab boycott could be Nestlé, the Swiss milk-products giant that owned 49 percent of L'Oréal and intended to become its majority stockholder. For Nestlé an Arab boycott could be disastrous. At least 15 percent of its exports were directed to the Arab countries. If L'Oréal wanted to keep Nestlé protected, it had to get the boycott lifted as soon as possible.

At first they tried bluster. On April 26, 1988, a bitter letter was sent by L'Oréal to the boycott commissioner general, Zouheir Akil, in Damascus. L'Oréal called the measures taken against it by the Boycott Bureau "surprising and inexplicable." Akil tartly answered, on June 5,

1988, that L'Oréal hadn't complied with the boycott regulations in spite of the grace periods the Boycott Bureau
had granted it.

There could be no mistake: L'Oréal had to adopt a
new strategy. The time when Castres Saint-Martin and
Sanchez alone could take care of the matter was over. An
unofficial steering committee was formed inside L'Oréal
to supervise the negotiations with the Arabs. Its main figure was Jacques Corrèze, who worked in close association
with Castres and Sanchez. According to L'Oréal documents, former president Dalle and vice president Lacharrière also were privy to some of the top-secret aspects of
the negotiation, especially the contacts concerning payoffs
to political figures in the Middle East.

But the payoff system hadn't worked, and Abdel Bari
had failed. L'Oréal had to recruit the best man in the field
to extract itself from the mess with the Arabs.

The company heads found the best man indeed: Ambassador Claude de Kemoularia.

Bald and thin, Claude de Kemoularia was a cultivated
and pleasant man. As a diplomat of the Fourth Republic,
he had worked with prominent statesmen and powerful
moguls. He had been the privy counselor to Prince Rainier
of Monaco. He had been an assistant to the United Nations
secretary general. He also had scores of Arab friends.

He had become a banker after de Gaulle's ascension
to power, but with Mitterrand's election he had turned
diplomat again. He had served as France's ambassador to
the Netherlands and to the United Nations. After his return
he had become an unofficial adviser to Mitterrand on Arab
affairs.

In 1981, before leaving for the Hague, Kemoularia
had been a member of the secret committee established

by François Mitterrand to prepare the new antiboycott policies. He had worked with Charles Salzmann, Professor Jean-Louis Bismuth, young economist Marc Boudier, and a few others. Mitterrand then sent Kemoularia to convince the Arab leaders that they had to accept the new French stance.

He did a marvelous job. First he visited the Arab embassies in Paris, in the company of Hubert Védrine, Mitterrand's diplomatic adviser. They explained the new policy on the Middle East to the Arab ambassadors, stressing that "close ties of France with Israel will help your interests." After the Élysée antiboycott committee completed its task, Kemoularia toured the Arab nations and met with their leaders. He made thirty-two trips to Arab capitals in the company of Marc Boudier.

His quiet efforts were fruitful, if only in the moderate Arab states. Kemoularia's trip to Saudi Arabia was particularly successful. From Riyadh he dispatched a telegram to President Mitterrand assuring him of King Khaled's friendship, and his excellent impression of their recent meeting in Paris. Kemoularia also quoted Prince Fahd, the future Saudi monarch, who expressed "his confidence in the French people."

"Kemoularia does these things very well," noted Jacques Attali, Mitterrand's adviser and confidant.

By 1988 Kemoularia had retired from the diplomatic service and was a consultant to several financial companies. His main activity was as a director of the Paribas bank. He had another position that was known to very few: he was president of a discreet organization called Club Péninsule Arabique. This Arabian Peninsula Club had been established, together with five others, by Prime Minister Michel Rocard in order to strengthen economic ties between France and several regions of the world.

Kemoularia's club included senior diplomats at the Quai d'Orsay—the ministry of foreign affairs—officials of the ministry for foreign trade, and businessmen. As its president he had visited several Arab countries in the past few years and maintained close relations, at the highest level, with their governments.

Kemoularia was a good friend of André Bettencourt, the majority owner of L'Oréal. The two men had met in the early fifties, when Kemoularia was chief of staff to vice premier Paul Reynaud and Bettencourt was a member of Parliament and a minister.

For all these reasons L'Oréal's masters decided to put Kemoularia in charge of their negotiations with the very same boycott institutions he had fought seven years before.

Kemoularia accepted the mission for L'Oréal, and at the end of June 1988 he flew to Damascus to meet with Zouheir Akil, the commissioner general of the Boycott Bureau. In spite of the fact that he was working for a private company, the French diplomats in Damascus received their prestigious former colleague warmly and invited him to stay at the ambassador's residence. The services of the embassy were also put at his disposal. The French diplomats in Damascus apparently didn't care that Kemoularia was about to flout the law they were supposed to protect. Not only didn't they care, they actually helped him do it.

Kemoularia met with Zouheir Akil in the offices of the central Boycott Bureau. Akil told him, in substance, that there still were some Helena Rubinstein companies in Europe and in Israel, and L'Oréal had two choices—either to sell all of the Helena Rubinstein companies it owned, or to buy the remaining Helena Rubinstein companies, including the Israeli one, replace their directors, and change their names. The Boycott Bureau would not agree to any other solution.

The main problem, Zouheir Akil explained, was Helena Rubinstein Israel, which was owned by the Israeli company Ossem and some individuals. L'Oréal had to find a way to make this company disappear.

Back in Paris, Kemoularia immediately wrote a mellifluous letter to Akil. The letter, dated July 4, 1988, was written on paper embossed with the L'Oréal letterhead and carried the inscription "Financial Committee."

In his letter Kemoularia effusively thanked Akil for "the quality of his welcome." He had informed L'Oréal's board of directors "about our conversations and about the measures that are recommended in order to obtain the cancellation of the boycott. I am delighted to inform you of the agreement of L'Oréal's general directorate to the suggestions I made to them following our conversation."

L'Oréal, Kemoularia went on, had decided to exercise the option allowing it to repurchase the totality of the Helena Rubinstein shares, thereby becoming the sole owner of the brand Helena Rubinstein and its commercial products in the world. This would happen by July 31, 1988. "I really wanted you to be the first informed about this acquisition," Kemoularia wrote.

Still, there was a problem with Helena Rubinstein Israel. Since it belonged to local interests, "it is, unfortunately, impossible for us to acquire it." Still, Kemoularia had a ready solution. He promised that L'Oréal would establish contact with the Israeli company and make it stop the manufacturing of Helena Rubinstein products by December 31, 1988, stop exporting Helena Rubinstein products from Israel, and change its name.

In other words, L'Oréal was yielding totally to the boycott.

"All this will show you, I believe," Kemoularia concluded, "that L'Oréal wishes to reach an agreement with the central Boycott Bureau and is taking all the necessary steps for that purpose."

Keeping its promise, L'Oréal immediately started a negotiation with HR Israel. A year earlier it had informed the Israeli company that L'Oréal was "reorganizing its activity" and eliminating most of the Helena Rubinstein plants in Europe. The factories in France, Italy, Great Britain, and Spain were to be closed, while a superfactory would be established in Erkrath, Germany, which would supply the new range of products to all local HR companies.

L'Oréal proposed that Israel join that new arrangement. The finished products imported from Germany would be top quality, and their cost to the Israelis would be much lower than that of manufacturing the same products at their plant in Galilee. But there was a condition attached. If Helena Rubinstein Israel wanted this tantalizing new deal, it had to change its name.

Why would anyone want to accept such a condition? Helena Rubinstein was a prestigious trademark. There had to be a powerful inducement to give up the name—and L'Oréal found one. It offered the Ossem company the agency of L'Oréal's products in Israel. The marketing of finished products wasn't affected by the Arab boycott. L'Oréal told the Israelis that if they represented other L'Oréal products, they couldn't market them under the name of Helena Rubinstein. They therefore had to change the company name.

L'Oréal did already have an agent in Israel, Efraim Apter, but it simply canceled the agreement with him. Apter wanted to sue, but he had very few documents attesting he was a direct agent of the firm, and he had to give up.

The main points of the deal offered to the Ossem company were the following: Helena Rubinstein Israel ceases to exist as such. It obtains the exclusive marketing of Helena Rubinstein products from Germany, and becomes the agent of L'Oréal and several other famous brands controlled by L'Oréal. In return, the owners of Helena Rubinstein Israel agree to change the name of their company.

The new name chosen was Interbeauty. The date set for the change was December 31, 1988.

And so, on October 26, 1988, L'Oréal sent a jubilant letter to the Boycott Bureau in Damascus, informing it that "the situation which caused [the boycott of L'Oréal] decision has already vanished, or else will be changed according to [your] wishes on December 31 midnight at the latest."

We have confirmed to the Israeli company that starting January 1, 1989, they will no longer have the right to manufacture the products, they will receive no more technical assistance or communication of know-how and will no longer have the right to use the brands of Helena Rubinstein. The Israeli company will only have the right to import from the Federal Republic of Germany and distribute in Israel the finished product, prepackaged and ready for sale. Moreover, they will be forbidden to export these products.

L'Oréal stressed how tough it was being with Israel. "None of the companies of the Helena Rubinstein group will be able in the future to take any decision related to Israel without having first received our agreement. . . . The Israeli company will be in breach with our own company in the event that they continue to manufacture the Helena Rubinstein products after December 31, 1988. Our company . . . would then take all legal steps necessary for the protection of its rights."

In that long letter L'Oréal also offered assurances that it had bought all the Helena Rubinstein companies throughout the world, as Kemoularia had promised.

We say again:

That no more subsidiaries of Helena Rubinstein exist in Israel.

That the manufacturing of the products will come to an end on December 31, 1988. We shall be vigilant on this.

That our company controls the companies and brands Helena Rubinstein in the whole world.

On November 24, 1988, soon after the mailing of that letter, Claude de Kemoularia and Pierre Castres Saint-Martin flew to Damascus and personally brought Zouheir Akil the voluminous file containing the proof of all the transactions, translated into Arabic and duly certified.

They returned to Paris in high spirits, and Kemoularia dispatched another letter to Akil: "You indicated to me that you were going to begin to study these files in the shortest possible time. I am convinced that this study will confirm to you that the company L'Oréal has indeed responded in a positive way to all your requests and that it has delivered all documents required by you." He signed the letter as "financial adviser" of L'Oréal.

It is pathetic to imagine Claude de Kemoularia, until recently a prestigious ambassador of France and architect of her antiboycott policies, zealously courting Zouheir Akil, a subordinate of Syrian intelligence, and expressing his readiness to bend to blackmail. Syria was, after all, a state supporting international terrorism, the headquarters of the ten bloodiest terrorist organizations of the world, for many years a refuge of the notorious Carlos, and still the sanctuary of Nazi criminals like Alois Brünner.

In his letter Kemoularia asked that the decree of boycott be annulled at the upcoming session of the Boycott Bureau's general assembly, scheduled for early January 1989.

The goal was in reach—yet somebody still had to go to Israel and finalize the deal in person, had to ensure that the owners of Helena Rubinstein Israel would sign the agreements certifying that they would stop production and change the company name. The trip to Israel was parallel, in a way, to Kemoularia's flights to Damascus. This was a very delicate mission, one on which the entire deal depended.

Nobody would have thought that the man who carried out the crucial negotiation would willingly do such a thing. He was the most unlikely person to volunteer for a trip to the Jewish state.

It was Jacques Corrèze.

9

The amiable elderly gentleman who came to Tel Aviv in late 1988 told his Israeli interlocutors that he was a great friend of Israel, but he asked them not to bruit his name about because "then he wouldn't be able to help anymore." He also said that he had visited the country briefly in the past, while on a Mediterranean cruise. To Gad Propper, Helena Rubinstein Israel's chairman of the board and major shareholder, he seemed to be "a charming person, who loved Israel." Propper found Corrèze "a big, charismatic man, a man who filled the room and made you want to be with him, to do great things with him."

To Eric Gornitzky, the company's lawyer, Corrèze confided that he was not proud of his past during World War II, but Gornitzky apparently had the tact not to ask embarrassing questions. It is clear, though, that he had no idea that the suave, soft-spoken Frenchman visiting his office was a hardened war criminal.

Corrèze knew he was taking a risk by visiting the State

of Israel, which had sworn to hunt down Nazi criminals and bring them to justice. Nonetheless, the Helena Rubinstein deal was of crucial importance to him. The long, difficult operation of buying out Helena Rubinstein through bogus companies around the world was nearing completion. This was to be the crowning success of his career, and he was ready even to go to Israel in order to achieve it.

Actually, Corrèze had been in charge of the negotiation with the Israelis from the start. "At L'Oréal there were two groups," he later said. "One was in charge of the Israelis, and that was my job; the other was in charge of the Arabs, and it was the task of Monsieur de Kemoularia."

In Israel, Corrèze met with Gornitzky and the top executives of HR Israel, headed by Gad Propper. He had already met a few of them in Europe. Ironically he had a good working relationship with Avraham Nussan, the HR Israel director, who was a death camp survivor. One can imagine Nussan's reaction if he had learned the real identity of his business associate.

In the negotiations Corrèze introduced himself as representative of the perfumes and cosmetics division of L'Oréal. He didn't mention his position at Helena Rubinstein. He said, though, that he had been a close friend of Madame Rubinstein.

Corrèze manipulated the Israelis with consummate slyness. They never suspected that the Arab boycott was the real motivation for L'Oréal's initiative and for the tempting benefits their guest dangled before their eyes. L'Oréal is going to make you its agent in Israel, Corrèze told Avraham Nussan. We'll give you the rights to sell Lancôme, Cacharel, Giorgio Armani, and other products of our group. But you can't do this as Helena Rubinstein.

These products don't belong to Helena Rubinstein. If you want to sell them, you must change your name.

Corrèze's arguments made sense. His arguments about the closing of the Helena Rubinstein production line were logical as well. The Israelis were impressed by his descriptions of the superfactory in Germany, which would bring down costs and improve quality. Besides, Gad Propper understood that Helena Rubinstein was changing its line of products, modifying formulas, labels, and packaging. He couldn't keep producing the old items, since they were being discontinued.

Propper and his associates therefore agreed to Corrèze's proposals and concluded several agreements with L'Oréal. Corrèze was the man who signed the papers in the name of L'Oréal, at Gornitzky's law office. On December 26, 1988, the executives of Helena Rubinstein Israel visited the Registrar of Companies at the Ministry of Justice and changed the name of their company to Interbeauty Inc.

Gad Propper later said, "Parallel to the talks with us, there were contacts behind my back. I was not aware of this. It seems a wife is always the last person to find out about her husband seeing another woman. . . . They did things we were not aware of with the boycott, and used the . . . reorganization for other objectives. We did not know that, at the time of the negotiation. Had we known they were in distress, we might have said that we didn't want any reorganization, and forced them to buy the factory for a lot of money! Twice its value! [But] they never offered to buy. They are excellent poker players."

A private detective hired by Jean Frydman's Israeli lawyer followed Corrèze's trail at Helena Rubinstein Israel. In his report, submitted a year later, he emphasized the warm relations between Corrèze and several Israeli executives; they asked, however, that Corrèze's name be kept secret, so he could continue to help Israel. "For me," an Israeli connected to the Propper company said, "Corrèze doesn't exist." A report from the U.S. also stressed that Corrèze was very discreet about his activities.

Jacques Corrèze returned from Tel Aviv to Paris with the freshly signed contracts with the Israelis in his brief-case. Everything was in order now, and the boycott was going to be lifted very soon. He had won.

Or so he thought.

Zouheir Akil was determined to make the L'Oréal ex-ecutives crawl on their bellies before he gave them what they wanted. For the following few months he barraged them with minutiae.

On December 13, he complained that he didn't have in his possession the papers certifying the name change of the Israeli company. This was only to be expected, since the official change would not occur until December 31. But Akil took the opportunity to humiliate the French company a little more. He wrote: "Despite your letter of 17 October 1988, addressed to the Israeli company . . . and their letter to you of 24 October 1988 . . . the said Israeli company is still bearing the name Helena Rubinstein." It was clear he wasn't going to lift the boy-cott before getting absolute proof that Helena Rubinstein Israel no longer existed.

He went even further, amassing a plethora of petty details. Going back in time to 1983, he wrote: "From the documents presented by you, the price of selling the shares owned by the Swiss company Helena Rubinstein AG in the Israeli company Helena Rubinstein Ltd. was U.S. $850,000 paid in three installments. . . . However, the bank documentation presented by you shows that the amounts paid to that Swiss company were as follows:

"U.S. $218,558 on 10 January 1983.

"U.S. $255,000 on 4 July 1983.

"U.S. $212,500 on 3 July 1984. [These amounts adding up to $686,058 only.] Therefore, please explain," the inquisitioner from Damascus wrote, "why the amounts actually paid were much less than those agreed upon, and present the documents evidencing the reduction of those amounts."

Akil then went into a detailed calculation of dividends and royalties paid by the Israelis since 1977, and demanded a full explanation and justification of each amount. He then scolded the L'Oréal executives for getting the contract with the Panamanians notarized at the Tunisian embassy in France instead of the Tunisian embassy in Switzerland(!), as well as for not certifying copies of checks with the right notaries and authorities in France or elsewhere, and for other peccadillos.

If he wanted to make L'Oréal sweat, he succeeded. In Clichy they knew that in a few days the boycott assembly would meet.

On December 30 a harried Castres Saint-Martin wrote to Akil, stressing that L'Oréal was "anxious to answer immediately the different points you raise. . . . We guarantee upon our honor that our declaration [about the name change of Helena Rubinstein Israel] is true, and that we shall send you as soon as possible the certificate by the Israel Register of Commerce." As far as the sums mentioned in Akil's letter were concerned, Castres Saint-Martin subserviently added and subtracted sums as small as $36,442 to show that his reports were correct. The letter was dispatched by overnight mail.

Yet the boycott master wasn't satisfied. He didn't answer Kemoularia's phone calls. He ignored an urgent telex from Castres Saint-Martin.

On January 3, Kemoularia sent another telex to the French embassy commercial attaché, Jean-François Riva-Roveda, asking him to meet with Zouheir Akil at once and convince him to clear L'Oréal. He now had proof of the name change of Helena Rubinstein Israel.

"We have been diligent," Kemoularia wrote, "and on January 3 at 13:05 we received by fax from Israel an extract from the Israeli Register of Companies, proving that the name 'Helena Rubinstein Limited' had been replaced by the new name 'Interbeauty Limited' on December 26, 1988, meaning five days earlier than the commitment we had made to the Boycott Bureau. . . . I hope that the central Boycott Bureau will take into consideration the efforts deployed by the L'Oréal company to fully answer [their] questions."

Once again the French embassy in Damascus assumed a dubious role, following the explicit orders of the foreign ministry and the ministry of trade. It actively assisted Kemoularia's efforts, and helped him prove to the boycott authorities that L'Oréal had indeed complied with their demands.

Following phone calls and telex messages from Kemoularia, Alain Grenier, the French ambassador to Syria, also called the commercial attaché and instructed him to request an immediate appointment with Zouheir Akil. Riva-Roveda received similar instructions from the Ministry of Foreign Trade in Paris. His superior there was Olivier Louis, the man in charge of the Third Subdirectorate, which dealt with the Middle East.

Besides his official functions in the ministry, Louis also was the secretary general of the Arabian Peninsula

Club. In addition, Louis was a friend of Marc Ladreit de Lacharrière, with whom he had studied at the École Nationale d'Administration. When questioned later, he confirmed that Ladreit de Lacharrière had spoken to him about the L'Oréal affair. Riva-Roveda confirmed that Louis was the man who gave him direct orders from Paris, although the two men had never met.

This was a typical old-boy network, centered around the Quai d'Orsay, the foreign ministry. All this web of friendships, business connections, official contacts, and unofficial complicities, permeated by the pro-Arab attitude of the Quai d'Orsay, had one result—the breaking of the law by the very branches of government charged with its enforcement.

Pressured by Kemoularia, and following the instructions of Ambassador Grenier, Riva-Roveda telephoned the boycott office and obtained an appointment with the boycott commissioner that same morning. Riva-Roveda hurried to the boycott office and conveyed Kemoularia's message to Zouheir Akil.

Akil told Riva-Roveda, "L'Oréal, in the shortest possible time, has submitted to the bureau a file whose quality the bureau appreciates. The bureau is also aware of the exceptional financial effort made by L'Oréal to satisfy the bureau's conditions.

"The last substantial question, namely the change of name of HR Israel, seems to have been solved (on condition that the necessary document be delivered to the bureau)."

Akil refused, however, to add the L'Oréal affair to the boycott assembly agenda of January 7, and required first the name-change documents and full answers to his last letter of December 13, 1988. On the other hand, he promised that L'Oréal's case would be examined at the next assembly session, in July. As soon as the decision was taken by the assembly, L'Oréal could "prepare the conditions of its return to the [Arab] markets."

Riva-Roveda returned to the embassy and wrote a detailed report. Ambassador Grenier immediately cabled the Quai d'Orsay, transmitting the entire report word for word, and asked that it be brought to the attention of Kemoularia.

This collusion between the embassy and L'Oréal's envoys made the French foreign ministry an accomplice in breaking French law. Years later, former planning minister Lionel Stoleru bitterly said:

"It is clear that L'Oréal acted wrongly. It is as clear that the Quai d'Orsay, by the intermediary of Mr. Claude de Kemoularia, played once again a totally negative role. The antiboycott cell created around Mr. Salzmann and Mr. de Kemoularia very quickly turned into a cell that took care of the affairs of Damascus. . . . The pro-Arab tradition of the ministry of foreign affairs . . . transformed this procedure into a system of negotiations with the Syrian capital. Besides, Kemoularia's notes are much worse than all the internal documents of L'Oréal."

On February 1, 1989, Castres Saint-Martin dispatched another letter to Zouheir Akil, which included all the needed attestations, official stamps, certified translations, and authorizations in twenty-five copies. He obediently detailed the transactions with HR Israel down to the last cent.

This diligence was being practiced, however, in tandem with a renewed effort, begun the year before, to bribe the leading boycott officials in the Middle East.

On August 31, 1988, several months after Kemoularia's first visit to Damascus, a secret meeting was held in

Paris. Jacques Corrèze, Gérard Sanchez, and two other L'Oréal executives met with Abdullah Abdel Bari. He was the Egyptian representative whom Sanchez had already contacted about setting up payoffs in the Middle East. He was also L'Oréal's informant about the inner machinery of the boycott.

After Kemoularia had begun negotiations with the Boycott Bureau in Damascus, some L'Oréal executives presumed that Abdel Bari's operation was at an end. But the Egyptian promptly informed them that it was too late to cancel the payoffs. If L'Oréal didn't honor its commitments, he said, the Arabs "would do anything" to prevent lifting their boycott. Besides, that might entail a danger for L'Oréal's "security" and for his own as well.

These hints, viewed against the backdrop of bloody terrorist attacks in the Middle East and Europe, had an ominous tone. Not long before, Arab terrorists masterminded by Iran had planted a bomb in the Tati department store in Paris. The explosion had wrought carnage: seven people killed, fifty wounded. Nobody wanted bombs to start exploding in L'Oréal's outlets around the world. Besides, it was suggested, Kemoularia's mission might end in failure, so L'Oréal had better pursue the payoff scheme as well.

Accordingly, on August 31, Abdel Bari came to Paris to plan the next step. The head of the L'Oréal secret group that met him was Jacques Corrèze. That is confirmed by the confidential report Sanchez wrote of the meeting, which ends with the words: "Mr. Corrèze repeated his orders to say nothing and do nothing."

Abdel Bari spoke at length, analyzing the situation. He stated his opinion that the boycott would finally be lifted, but certainly not by February 1989. Still, that would depend on the people with the real power behind the Damascus Boycott Bureau. "In Damascus," he said, "we play with loaded dice. We believe we are talking with Zouheir Akil, but the man behind him is Abu Rami."

He was referring to one of the chiefs of Syrian intelligence, and the head of Syria's secret operations in Europe, whose real name was Mohammed Makhlouf. The brother-in-law of President Assad, he controlled the Damascus regional Boycott Bureau. Abdel Bari stated that Abu Rami had "the power of life and death" over Zouheir Akil.

He suggested two courses of action. The first was to bribe Abu Rami, having the payment also include a payoff for Zouheir Akil. The second was to establish a "counterpower" to the Syrians by recruiting the support of the Saudis.

Abdel Bari explained that if the regional Boycott Bureau in Jidda, Saudi Arabia, supported L'Oréal, it might neutralize the Syrians when the boycott assembly met. Abdel Bari suggested that L'Oréal send its file concerning the boycott to the Saudis, so they could force the Syrians to behave more sensibly at the next assembly meeting.

At a previous meeting Abdel Bari had identified his contact in Saudi Arabia as Sheikh Sabri Gabel, who would be ready to help for a bribe. At the August 31 meeting, however, Abdel Bari told his French friends that he wanted to discard the sheikh, who was not reliable. Instead, he mentioned two Saudi princes. Their names and functions were so secret that Gérard Sanchez didn't include them in his report and mentioned them only in a handwritten note he personally gave to his superiors.

The document reads like the premise of a cheap thriller.

NEW SAUDI CHANNEL OF M. ABDEL BARI

Prince Fahd has 7 brothers (children of the same Queen Mother) one of whom, Prince Turki, is his adviser specifically in matters of defense.

Turki is a close friend of Khaled, prince of a collateral branch of the Ibn Saud family. Khaled is the boss of the Saudi Secret Services operating in Europe and for this reason is in close relation with his Syrian opposite number Abu Rami.

Abdel Bari got in touch with Turki as well as with Khaled and spoke to them about our case. They are very well disposed toward us and Khaled would be ready, if asked by Abdel Bari, to replace Sheikh Sabri Gabel for our problem with Abu Rami (payments).

Abdel Bari was thus proposing that L'Oréal bribe two major Arab spymasters. This was hardly a job for perfume makers.

Sanchez was rather skeptical about the "Saudi channel." In his view, if L'Oréal's double game with the Syrians and the Saudis was exposed, the Boycott Bureau might become angry and everything could be lost. He preferred to give a free hand to Kemoularia in Damascus. Still, he suggested that they let Abdel Bari prepare his "Saudi safety net" but activate it only on L'Oréal's instructions.

Corrèze also preferred waiting to openly anti-Syrian activity. His instructions figured at the end of Sanchez's report of the meeting, a report addressed to the two men who had to make the decision in the name of L'Oréal: Castres Saint-Martin and Lacharrière.

During the following months several more meetings were held with Abdel Bari. The participants were Jacques

Corrèze, Claude de Kemoularia, François Dalle, Lacharrière, and Castres. The reason for these subsequent meetings was to nail down the lifting of the boycott—with hard cash.

On March 6, 1989, Abdel Bari informed Castres and Lacharrière by fax that the L'Oréal documents had been accepted by the Damascus regional bureau. The decision to lift the boycott would be made at the July 1989 semi-annual boycott assembly, attended by the representatives of all twenty-four regional offices.

Abdel Bari still believed, though, that the promises of payoffs would play an important part in the conclusion of the affair. He added that he had been closely followed and even pursued by his "contacts in Damascus, London, and Jidda" in order to make him "confirm commitments, guarantees, obligations, and promises of L'Oréal and myself."

He added that his contacts "demanded a written commitment from L'Oréal, attesting that our joint pledges will be honored. I told them that they should take my word, and that I already had received L'Oréal's promise. I answered in that way . . . in order to keep them under control and because of the 'low profile' that we decided to keep; and in order to avoid trouble or a hostile attitude by Abu Rami, which could compromise the positive results that were obtained. This follows your instructions, strategy, and tactics (Mr. Ambassador, Mr. Corrèze, Mr. Dalle and yourselves [Castres Saint-Martin and Ladreit de Lacharrière], following our large meeting at L'Oréal and the following meetings that took place afterward)."

Before the boycott was lifted, L'Oréal indeed had to pay. On May 4, 5, and 6, 1989, Abdel Bari met with the "middlemen" in Jidda to agree upon the bribes to be paid. Abu Rami's representative, Waki Allah, asked for $1.5

million; Sheikh Sabri Gabel was more modest and was ready to settle for a half million. Abdel Bari replied that L'Oréal wouldn't pay more than a million. His contact at L'Oréal, Gérard Sanchez, informed Castres, Corrèze, and Lacharrière about the negotiation, and it was decided to finalize the affair when Abdel Bari visited Paris on May 22.

It is not known exactly how much money was finally paid. Still, the bribes were at least a million dollars, as L'Oréal would admit two years later. According to a reliable source within the company, the payoffs totaled more than $2 million.

On July 22, 1989, Zouheir Akil sent an official letter to L'Oréal:

> We have the pleasure to inform you that the Arab boycott authorities, taking into consideration the documents presented by you, resolved to remove the ban imposed on your company and all its subsidiaries—including the American company Helena Rubinstein Inc. and all its subsidiaries—so that you are now in a position to resume trade with the Arab countries.
>
> While advising you of the above, we wish to your company, in its future dealings with the Arab countries, continuing development and prosperity.

10

Judge Getti expected the raid on L'Oréal to be extensively reported in the press, and he feared that the sensational coverage might obstruct the investigation. For six weeks, however, there was total silence. Strangely, the news of the gendarmerie raid on L'Oréal didn't leak to the media. Then, on May 6, 1991, the first article appeared in *Le Point*, a weekly newsmagazine. It triggered an avalanche.

In the following days the scandal exploded in front-page headlines all over the major French and international newspapers. Voluminous articles described in detail the raid on L'Oréal, the discovery of documents on the boycott, and Jacques Corrèze's role in the affair and his murky past. The slant of some articles was that L'Oréal hadn't acted differently from other French companies that also had complied with the boycott requirements; it had just been caught red-handed.

People learned sordid truths about the Boycott Bureau. Some of the boycott activities were frightening, others stupid, even ridiculous. The press reported that, besides hundreds of companies, the boycott's blacklist included institutions like Yale University, which had been banned by the Arab League because its coat of arms included Hebrew letters. Walt Disney's *Snow White and the Seven Dwarfs* was boycotted because the horse in the movie was called Samson. So was the slaves' chorus in Verdi's opera *Nabucco*, since the slaves happened to be Jewish. Emil Zola's novels were blacklisted as well. His crime was his famous newspaper article *"J'accuse"* in which he passionately defended the unjustly convicted Captain Alfred Dreyfus.

Annette Lévy-Willard of *Libération* unearthed incriminating material about Corrèze seizing Jewish property during the war. A savvy TV reporter for state-owned TF1, Françoise-Marie Morel, succeeded in entering Corrèze's apartment building, sticking her foot in the door and pointing her microphone at the reluctant octogenarian. Corrèze greeted the young woman politely but refused to speak about his past. *Le Monde*, France's most prestigious newspaper, published a series of articles about the boycott and L'Oréal. Magazines and weekend supplements delved again into the infamous history of La Cagoule and the collaboration with the Nazis.

In the onslaught most of the press reported Jean Frydman's accusations that L'Oréal harbored Nazi criminals. L'Oréal, highly embarrassed, accused Frydman of instigating the media campaign. Frydman held his ground: not only Corrèze but other notorious French Nazis, who had vanished since the war, had found refuge in L'Oréal's subsidiaries in Spain and South America.

When the affair first exploded in the papers, Jean Frydman was in Israel. Jean-Marie Pontaut of *Le Point* flew to Tel Aviv and was the first to interview Frydman.

"François Dalle was my friend," Frydman told him.
"How could he conceal from me the existence of a Corrèze? I consider this insupportable. By making my path
cross with a man emerging from Hell, forty years later,
he inevitably created a charged situation."

Eric Conan of the rival weekly *L'Express* interviewed
François Dalle. "This is disgusting financial blackmail,"
Dalle thundered. "Frydman is using the Holocaust to
make money, that's all!"

Dalle certainly wasn't an anti-Semite, but his outburst
had an ugly ring that tainted many of the articles inspired
by L'Oréal sources. Money, L'Oréal repeated; all the Frydmans wanted was money. L'Oréal wasn't anti-Semitic,
they pointed out; some of its top executives were Jewish.
Still, the response of L'Oréal and Dalle to Frydman's accusations played on the stereotype of the greedy Jew.

Jean Frydman, Dalle said in substance, only wanted
to get more money for his Paravision stock. "Since December 1989," Dalle said in a statement to the press,
"Jean Frydman has been waging a campaign whose only
goal is to force L'Oréal to buy his shares, which already
are overvalued, at a totally unrealistic price. . . . I am
deeply shocked and saddened by the statements of Mr.
Jean Frydman in the press, mostly made up of untruths or
combinations of unrelated matters, which is a particularly
insidious technique."

Le Monde too hinted that Frydman's motives were
financial. In a half-page article entitled "The Good Bargains of Paravision," the paper described the handsome
profits the Frydman brothers had made by selling their old
movies to L'Oréal, and stated that Mayoux's assessment
of the value of their shares was more than generous.
(Mayoux hadn't been found guilty of fraud yet.)

Lindsay Owen-Jones, L'Oréal's president, voiced similar arguments. At the general shareholders' assembly the young Welshman declared: "When we created Paravision . . . Jean Frydman brought a film library, for which he received twenty-five percent of Paravision's capital stock. But very soon doubts were raised about the value and the extent of the rights for this library. We had to part, but we had to buy Frydman's share."

This was a misrepresentation of the facts. The "doubts" Owen-Jones mentioned had nothing to do with the present crisis. He was mixing two wholly separate matters. It was true that some L'Oréal executives were not happy with the deal that the Frydman brothers had struck with them in 1988 when they had created Paravision. They believed that the price paid for the Frydmans' movie library—395 million francs (about $60 million)—had been exceedingly high. Most of the Frydman films were black and white, and despite the artistic value of movies like *Citizen Kane* and *High Noon*, they were not what the industry called "locomotives," meaning films that would be the main attraction in packages offered to prospective buyers. A movie like *Rambo*, or any other major Sylvester Stallone, Arnold Schwarzenegger, or Bruce Willis movie was such a locomotive. A classic like *The Bridge on the River Kwai* could also be one.

Some Paravision executives, like secretary general Raphael Berdugo, stressed that the film rights Paravision had acquired from the Frydman brothers allowed only television, not theater, screenings. In addition, many important countries like Germany, Italy, the U.K., Japan, and Australia were not included. Berdugo also believed that Jean Frydman was overly optimistic about Paravision's prospects. He assumed that François Dalle shared his feelings and for that reason had finally retreated from the Columbia buyout project.

Although L'Oréal might well have had grievances about the Paravision deal, it had never expressed them before and had never raised the subject with Jean Frydman. In any case, L'Oréal's grievances were irrelevant. The reason for Frydman's ouster from the Paravision board had been the boycott.

None of L'Oréal's top executives ever suggested ending the association with the Frydmans. Nor could anyone deny that on October 16, 1989, Paravision had done its best to reinstate Frydman as a member of the board. At no time during all that period did Dalle or anybody else mention any other cause besides the boycott for a temporary separation from Frydman. And it had been Frydman, not Dalle, who asked to part ways after finding out about Jacques Corrèze.

At the L'Oréal shareholders' general assembly, Owen-Jones went on to make another statement that didn't correspond to the facts. "[Corrèze] was seventy-eight when the [boycott affair] took place, and although being president of Cosmair, he didn't hold any operational role in the company, only an honorary position." Perhaps he wasn't aware of the very active role of Corrèze in the boycott affair—his participation in the discussion of the payoffs, his "orders" recorded by Sanchez, and his trips to Israel, where he had signed the new contracts on behalf of L'Oréal.

A third Owen-Jones declaration concerned the boycott itself: "We didn't submit to the pressure of the Arab League for a boycott of Israel," said the handsome young president. "After we acquired Helena Rubinstein, the Damascus authorities thought that we had a subsidiary in Israel that produced Helena Rubinstein cosmetics. These two facts were untrue. We turned to Claude de Kemou-laria, the ambassador of France at the United Nations. He notified Damascus that these pieces of information were false. The boycott of L'Oréal by the Arab countries had no more grounds. At the end of 1988, the Arab League informed us of its decision not to boycott us anymore."

Owen-Jones was cheered by his audience. If he had read the documents seized by Getti, though, L'Oréal's president probably would have made a different speech.

Judge Getti wanted to fly to New York and seize relevant documents from the Cosmair offices on Fifth Avenue, but his request for a trip to the United States vanished somewhere in the labyrinths of power. He never received an answer, never found out which authority had blocked his request. The *juge d'instruction* therefore lost a unique opportunity.

Corrèze remained an enigma. As the storm raged around him, the ailing old man remained a recluse in his superb flat overlooking the river Seine. He refused most interviews. The few people who caught a glimpse of him perceived a bald, frail man with sallow skin and sagging cheeks, who moved with difficulty, breathing through a plastic tube connected to an oxygen bottle. A Jewish businessman, Maurice Kahan, who had volunteered to investigate Corrèze, rang his bell and tried to ask a few questions, but the old man slammed the door in his face.

One of Corrèze's rare interviews was published by *Le Monde*, and its tone was sympathetic. Corrèze admitted he had visited Tel Aviv for talks with the owners of Helena Rubinstein Israel. "They know all about my past," he said. "They are delightful people." He also denied having taken part in any anti-Jewish activities during the war. He admitted that the organization of which he was a leader was fervently anti-Semitic, "but I was not involved in any abuse of the Jews, no, that's something completely different!"

Because the old man's health was getting worse, Judge Getti decided to interrogate him at home. On June 18 he came with his assistant, Mr. Faure, and was met by Corrèze and his lawyer, Guy Danet. Corrèze had difficulty speaking, but despite the fragile appearance, the oxygen tubes, the cancer-ridden flesh, Getti found a core of steel. Corrèze had been a tough fighter all his life, and he was not going to make any revelations that could harm his friends or the company that had made him a rich and powerful man. His brief testimony didn't disclose anything. "Cosmair," he said calmly, "has nothing to do with Helena Rubinstein or L'Oréal. . . . There is no legal connection between Helena Rubinstein and L'Oréal," and therefore "it is difficult to suppose that L'Oréal could be boycotted by the Arab League because of Helena Rubinstein."

Judge Getti asked him about his role in the boycott affair, but hit a brick wall again. "I knew Mr. Abdel Bari, who had worked for L'Oréal for about twenty years, so I had the opportunity to meet him a few times without any active participation on my side. . . . I never spoke of the boycott with Mr. Ladreit de Lacharrière. . . . I had the opportunity to meet Mr. Abdel Bari and Ladreit de Lacharrière, but we didn't discuss the boycott, we had conversations of a general nature." He didn't say a word about the payoffs to the Syrians and the Saudis, or about the orders he had given Sanchez and others concerning the negotiations with the Boycott Bureau.

He also denied any involvement in Jean Frydman's ouster from Paravision. He didn't know him, he didn't have an opinion of him, and he had no reason to have

Jean Frydman or anybody else evicted from Paravision.

Corrèze grudgingly recognized that François Dalle had spoken to him "incidentally" about the boycott. But only after being confronted with several documents from L'Oréal's archives did he admit having been involved in the affair. "There were two groups," he said. "One that dealt with the Israelis, and I was in charge, and the second that dealt with the Arabs, and that was de Kemoularia's job."

Why did he get involved? "Because I am the one who introduced Madame Helena Rubinstein to L'Oréal and because I am Rubinstein's agent in Spain."

Judge Getti left Corrèze's apartment disappointed. The man was tough, and there was nothing that could make him reveal his secrets.

That same day, however, a dramatic development cast new light on Jacques Corrèze.

When Jean Frydman had contacted Serge Klarsfeld two years before and asked him about Corrèze, the Nazi hunter's response had been lukewarm. He was surprised that Corrèze had climbed so high at L'Oréal, but he didn't consider Corrèze an important criminal. He knew he had been a Cagoule activist and Deloncle's confidant. On the other hand, if he had been released from jail, there was no reason why he shouldn't be allowed to start a new life. To a television reporter who interviewed him shortly after Corrèze's name had surfaced, Klarsfeld said, "I don't think he was big game."

Klarsfeld, a plump, white-haired lawyer, was the son of a Jew executed in Auschwitz for daring to slap back a guard who had beaten him up. His German-born wife, Beate, had been sentenced to a year in jail for publicly slapping German prime minister Kurt Georg Kiesinger; she did it to protest the fact that Kiesinger, a former Nazi official, could become prime minister in postwar Germany.

Serge Klarsfeld was the founder and president of the Organization of Sons and Daughters of Deported Jews in France. He published detailed records of the trainloads of French Jews sent to their death thanks to the Vichy government's cooperation with the Nazis. In 1991 Klarsfeld discovered, in a government archive, a detailed card index of the Jews of France, established by Vichy officials but devotedly preserved by diligent civil servants under all the subsequent French governments.

Even when the name of Corrèze first appeared in the French press, in May 1991, Klarsfeld remained reserved. But on June 6, when he read the *Le Monde* article about "The Good Bargains of Paravision" suggesting Frydman was solely concerned with money, he became very angry.

"I knew who Frydman was, after all. I knew he had participated in the first protest against the Nazis when he still was a kid. I knew he had been a real Resistance member, I knew he had been in Fresnes prison. I knew he had jumped off the deportation train. I knew his mother had been sent to a concentration camp. . . . Why should a man like him be instantly accused of making money from the Holocaust?

"If Frydman is also involved in a commercial conflict, does it necessarily mean that his motive must be money? I said to myself, this is another kind of anti-Semitism, which was also shared by a part of the Jewish elite. I saw that people belonging to the cream of the Jewish community also were complaining about Frydman's campaign. They didn't like what he was doing.

"That made me very angry, so I decided to review the Corrèze case. The press stressed that 'Corrèze had never done anything against the Jews.' So I started reviewing old material. First, I read my files on the bombing of the synagogues in November 1941, but Corrèze wasn't mentioned, of course. He was in Russia at that time, fighting the Bolsheviks. I continued my research at the Center of Contemporary Jewish Documentation, and I found a file I had put aside twenty years ago. At that time I was a member of the executive committee of LICRA, the League Against Racism and Anti-Semitism [originally called LICA], and I had collected documents about the illegal seizure of the LICA offices by Deloncle's MSR movement.

"I opened the file, and there was the name of Colonel Corrèze."

On March 25, 1941, Eugène Deloncle, the founder of La Cagoule and now the leader of the Mouvement Social Révolutionnaire, informed his Paris-based activists of a forthcoming operation: the seizure of six buildings belonging to French Jews. Deloncle wanted his men to feel that they were actively participating in cleansing Paris of Jews. He intended to use the buildings as offices and centers of his organization. The buildings were:

1. 83 avenue de la Grande-Armée, the headquarters of the World Jewish Congress
2. 67 avenue Victor-Hugo, the home of a Jewish former minister, Georges Mandel
3. 57 rue La Boétie, the home of the Wildenstein family
4. 17 rue Desbordes-Valmore, the store of Mr. Bernheim
5. 141 boulevard Haussmann, the offices of Bacry Brothers

6. 40 rue de Paradis, headquarters of the League
   Against Racism and Anti-Semitism (LICA)

The seizure of two other buildings, the Jewish Immigration Center and the Jewish Community headquarters,
was deferred.

The operation was coordinated with the German Kom-
mandantur, but not with the French police, which Deloncle treated with disdain. He knew well that his connections
in high places would thwart any police interference with
his operation. It was originally scheduled for March 26,
1941, but was put off until April 9. In a letter under the
heading "Order 22" Deloncle informed two chiefs of his
uniformed Légion Nationale Populaire that they would be
in charge of the operation. The designated chiefs were
Corrèze and Jacques Fauran.

Corrèze was put in charge of the First Sector—central
Paris—and his command post was established at RNP
headquarters on rue du Faubourg Saint-Honoré. Deloncle
appointed as his personal assistant in this operation the
notorious killer Jean Filliol, the same person who had
murdered the Rosselli brothers under the orders of Corrèze
four years before. Filliol, too, held the rank of colonel in
the Legion.

The seizures were carried out over three days in a
paramilitary operation with advance headquarters, command posts, and backup forces. The men were well armed.
The units involved reported to their district commanders
at regular intervals, describing in detail the seizure of the
buildings, the inventory of the furniture and other property
found inside, the reactions of neighbors, janitors, and police officers. Locksmiths arrived at the premises to change
the locks, bailiffs noted down the transfer of the property

to Deloncle's troops, and sentries were placed outside the occupied buildings.

The police turned out to be the main obstacle, interfering in several instances and even taking some of the Legionnaires into custody. Legally, the police had full authority to stop the men. But Deloncle and Corrèze had a solid network of conspirators, and their men didn't spend more than a few hours in a police station. The Délégation Gouvernementale pour les Territoires Occupés, which represented Vichy in the northern zone, ordered the police authorities not to intervene.

The field commanders' reports described the seizures as great patriotic deeds. The commander of the team that occupied the LICA building solemnly reported, "The concierge manifested her joy to see Frenchmen take possession of the place instead of Jews." That building was soon to become the headquarters of the Legion.

The commander of the Third District, one Gaudin, reported to Corrèze that while he was occupying the home of Georges Mandel, the police tried to interfere. Gaudin was briefly arrested, using the time for "propaganda before seven police officers belonging to the Judeo-Masonic trash, but not for long." After his release he occupied the home of the *youtre* ("hymie") and concluded: "This was a beautiful day for the real revolution, and the resurrection of the real France."

Corrèze was very active in the proceedings. He supervised his different teams, rushed to inspect the buildings newly conquered by his armed riffraff, and intervened when the police or other officials tried to halt the seizures. He received written reports from his district commanders. In one case he severely reprimanded a subordinate, the chief of the Fifth District, Michel Harispe. Harispe, who already enjoyed a sordid reputation in the

MSR (and who would die in prison a few years later), apparently hadn't sent a report of his operation to Corrèze's headquarters, and the angry colonel warned him in an official letter that he had to follow the orders of his superior officers.

The operation was completed on April 11. It was a total success.

The file discovered by Klarsfeld was corroborated by evidence already obtained by Annette Lévy-Willard, the reporter at *Libération*. She had found a complaint which Mr. Bernheim, the owner of the rue Desbordes-Valmore store, had filed with the Paris police, accusing Corrèze of looting. Lévy-Willard also found an impoundment order, signed by Corrèze, that the Legionnaires had displayed when trying to expel the Jewish owner of another store at 47 avenue d'Orléans. That meant Corrèze and his men had looted and seized other Jewish property besides the houses mentioned in Klarsfeld's file.

Serge Klarsfeld also discovered evidence that Corrèze had represented the MSR, together with Deloncle and Filliol, at the anti-Jewish exhibit held at the Palais Berlitz in Paris. The exhibit, depicting the Jews as despicable and inferior, had been organized by the Propaganda Staffel and the Department of Jewish Questions.

The documents obtained by Klarsfeld changed his mind. Corrèze had actively participated in acts of persecution against the Jews during the war. Klarsfeld dispatched an urgent request to Neil Sher, director of the Office of Special Investigations of the United States Justice Department. He asked that Jacques Corrèze be placed on the "watch list" and forbidden to enter the United States.

The watch list had become famous recently when U.S. immigration authorities had written on it the name of Kurt

Waldheim, the president of Austria. Waldheim, who had served earlier as secretary general of the United Nations, had been exposed as a Wehrmacht officer whose unit had taken part in war crimes in the Balkans. The evidence about his questionable past, which included documents and photographs, had been found in a file kept, oddly enough, in the cellars of the UN building in New York. Serge Klarsfeld and his wife had been very active in the campaign to banish Kurt Waldheim.

As Corrèze took center stage, the L'Oréal affair hit the major U.S. newspapers. On June 7, 1991, the *Wall Street Journal* titled its front-page article "Ordeal Has L'Oréal Wishing Mr. Frydman Would Take a Powder." The detailed article noted: "This is the kind of intense, messy *affaire* that occasionally grips France, which has never resolved its guilt over its World War II occupation by Germany." The *New York Times* published a long dispatch from Paris under the headline "L'Oréal Official Investigated by U.S. Over Pro-Nazi Past."

The French media reacted strongly to the new revelations. *Le Monde*, which had published its sympathetic profile of Corrèze only a few days before, quoted again his declaration that he hadn't done anything against the Jews, and noted: "The documents produced today by Mr. Klarsfeld prove at least that Mr. Jacques Corrèze . . . has set for himself some quite convenient memory lapses." On June 20, 1991, Corrèze reluctantly admitted on Channel 5 of French television that the documents discovered by Klarsfeld "couldn't be invented" and said that he regretted "having done, during his actions in that period for a laudable goal, things that could have inconvenienced other human beings."

"Do you feel you were a real anti-Semite?" the reporter asked.

"I don't know if I was, but I'm about to become one," was the answer.

Jean-Pierre Meyers, André Bettencourt's son-in-law, who had earlier dismissed the charges against Corrèze, came secretly to meet with Serge Klarsfeld. He was accompanied by his uncle, Rabbi David Liché, and asked to see the documents about Corrèze. "It's annoying," he admitted. "Corrèze had sworn to us he had never done anything against the Jews." He asked for Klarsfeld's advice.

"Get rid of him as soon as possible," Klarsfeld firmly said. "He lied to you, so get rid of him!"

A Nestlé official hurriedly declared that when the company acquired majority control of Cosmair in 1984, it had known nothing about Corrèze's pro-Nazi past.

Still, L'Oréal kept supporting Corrèze. A spokesman told the *New York Times*, "In light of Mr. Corrèze's weak physical condition and contribution to Cosmair, L'Oréal does not intend to ask him to step down." The spokesman vigorously denied that L'Oréal or Cosmair was anti-Semitic. They stressed that Owen-Jones's predecessor as president of L'Oréal, Charles Zwiac, had been Jewish and several of his relatives had died in concentration camps.

Owen-Jones added, "This is not a guy who tried to hide in Argentina or Brazil. He never changed his name. He has been punished."

This was his official position. But behind the scenes he was having second thoughts. He had a long conversation with Maurice Lévy, the director of Publicis, France's largest advertising agency and also L'Oréal's public relations firm. Until now Lévy had supported wholeheartedly L'Oréal's hostility toward Jean Frydman. At this point, though, he was compelled to take action. He and Owen-Jones went to André Bettencourt, L'Oréal's owner, and convinced him to get rid of Corrèze. According to certain sources, the conversation was so heated that both Lévy and Owen-Jones threatened to resign if Corrèze was not fired. After their meeting, one of the participants told some of his friends that "he had got Corrèze's head."

In the meantime, Corrèze had been rushed to the American Hospital in Neuilly. His cancer of the pancreas had reached a terminal stage. On June 26, 1991, L'Oréal's executives hurried to the hospital and made him sign a letter of resignation on his deathbed.

"As I am facing the development of a controversy that concerns only me, but which might cause harm to the Cosmair company, and considering my poor health, I believe it is my duty to ask to be discharged of my functions of chairman (honorary president) and member of the board of this company," the letter stated.

Corrèze admitted that he was "in the center of a controversy concerning his past," and added, "I want to point out that my activities before the war and during the occupation, including the facts most recently reported by the press, have already cost me trials and sentences to ten years in jail. In 1959, I was granted a personal amnesty, followed by a rehabilitation in November 1966.

"I cannot change what has been. Allow me simply to express my most heartfelt and sincere regrets for the acts that I may have committed forty years ago, and their consequences, even if indirect."

Corrèze also addressed the Paravision affair: "I wish to state with the utmost firmness that I am not concerned in any way . . . with the audiovisual subsidiary of L'Oréal, Paravision, or with the conflict between this company and Mr. Jean Frydman, whom I don't know and about whom I've never been asked to express any opinion.

"The accusations of Mr. Frydman against me stem therefore from a totally unjustified and artificial mixture of unconnected matters. The French judiciary will decide on that issue."

It can be assumed that Corrèze hadn't written his statement but merely signed it. When questioned, L'Oréal executives confirmed that Corrèze's letter was "a personal decision, taken in agreement with the management of L'Oréal."

L'Oréal was hurriedly distancing itself from Corrèze. That same day, in an interview with *Time* magazine, unnamed L'Oréal officials departed from the position established in the past by François Dalle and confirmed that the company founder, Eugène Schueller, "was an anti-Semitic fascist who had hired Corrèze and other right-wing extremists."

Three hours after his resignation letter reached the news agencies, Jacques Corrèze died—rather conveniently for some people. A rumor quickly spread in Paris hinting that Corrèze couldn't have written and signed his letter at all, since he apparently had been in a coma for the last day of his life.

Jean and David Frydman obtained a copy of the resignation letter and submitted it to a graphology expert, Marie-Jeanne Berrichon-Sedeyn. Her five-page report stated:

Even though the signature in question was examined only on a telefax, which doesn't allow a sharp scrutiny, [I] have found important differences between this signature and uncontested samples that originated from Mr. Corrèze. These differences, concerning simultaneously the proportions, the disposition of three elements of the signature in regard to each other, and the morphology of each of these elements, cast a very serious doubt on the authenticity of this signature.

It seems likely that an examination of the original will allow one to conclude that it is a forgery, executed by a person who imitated samples [of the signature]."

L'Oréal's executives indignantly rejected the allegations both that Corrèze's letter had not been signed by him and that it had been released to the press shortly before his death without his knowledge.

A last mystery had been added to Jacques Corrèze's stormy life.

11

Corrèze was dead, but the L'Oréal affair was far from over.

On April 11, 1991, barely two weeks after the raid on L'Oréal and two months before Corrèze's name would create world headlines, Judge Getti and his assistants had started interrogating the *dramatis personae* of the affair. After studying the sworn statements of the Frydman brothers, Getti decided to obtain further testimony about the fictitious board meeting of March 30, 1989.

He first interviewed Catherine Morisse, Paravision's former legal adviser. She described to him the way she had established the legal account of the board meeting that never was, following the instructions of her president, Michel Pietrini. The young woman declared that she had prepared the papers, convinced that Frydman had resigned, as she had been told. Although she was a close family friend of Jean Frydman's, it had never crossed her mind to talk to him about his sudden resignation. She didn't see him often, since he spent most of his time in Canada and Israel, she said. She also believed she had to be loyal to her president, and didn't think it was proper to tell other people about matters Michel Pietrini had discussed with her.

The following day, Getti's gendarmes interrogated the lawyers Legros and Duprez, the heads of the Clavier legal firm. Three days later they summoned Janine Lorck, Catherine Morisse's assistant. At the end of these interrogations Getti had established that the March 30, 1989, board meeting at which Frydman had allegedly resigned had been held on paper only, that there had been no letter of resignation by Jean Frydman, and that the information given the Tribunal de Commerce was false.

Getti now turned to a second category of witnesses: Paravision's top officials, the members of the board and the strategic committee. On April 15, 1991, the investigators questioned Raphael Berdugo, Paravision's secretary general. Berdugo described his doubts about the real value of Frydman's film library, an interesting but irrelevant observation.

Later that day, Jean-Pierre Meyers came to the gendarmes' shabby office in the Marais. The husband of Eugène Schueller's granddaughter, a handsome, balding man in his early forties, had harsh words for Frydman.

"He is a blackmailer," Meyers said. "He tries to drape his exit from Paravision in moral motives, but in reality his behavior . . . shows clearly that he is motivated by material considerations. . . . All this business is finally an affair of big money. . . . I can't accept [Frydman's] accusations that we didn't behave properly toward him from a moral point of view, in particular in matters of discrimination. I am a Jew myself. . . . My grandparents were deported to Auschwitz. My grandfather was a rabbi, he was the first to be deported."

Boycott? No, Meyers hadn't been involved in any discussions about the boycott.

Corrèze? He didn't mention the name.

Jean Frydman's resignation? "He resigned in March."

How did Meyers know? "François Dalle told me."

At his interview on May 3, 1991, Lindsay Owen-Jones was so detached, he could have been a United Nations observer. L'Oréal's president declared that he had agreed to establish Paravision at François Dalle's suggestion, hinting that because of Dalle's position at L'Oréal, he actually had no choice. He and L'Oréal didn't know anything about Paravision, except for consolidating its budget. He had been kept out of the management and the administration of Paravision. He had never attended a Paravision board meeting, and he had never been asked for advice. He had met Jean Frydman only once.

The boycott? Paravision had nothing to do with it. Owen-Jones suggested that Getti's men should direct their questions concerning the boycott to Castres Saint-Martin. Corrèze? He had not been directly involved with the boycott, and his name had been mentioned only because François Dalle had appointed him honorary president of Helena Rubinstein.

On May 10, 1991, Pierre Castres Saint-Martin calmly declared that as financial director of L'Oréal he was in charge only of the treasury. "Concerning the negotiations with the boycott offices, the general management of L'Oréal had chosen external consultants to carry them through, and I was in charge of the liaison between the general management and these consultants."

He had apparently forgotten the extensive correspondence between him and the boycott bureau during the years 1986–89. Or perhaps he didn't know that Getti had found in L'Oréal's files at least eight letters and declarations bearing his signature and addressed to Mohammed el-Ajami and Zouheir Akil in Damascus.

Castres Saint-Martin claimed that Abdel Bari had been an "external consultant" who carried on the negotiations with the Boycott Bureau on behalf of L'Oréal. After Abdel Bari's failure, he said, he had been replaced by Claude de Kemoularia.

Helena Rubinstein Israel? Castres had negotiated with Gad Propper, the major shareholder, and Avraham Nussan, the director general, with the help of Jacques Corrèze. The Israelis themselves had asked to stop production and had decided to close their factory in 1987. This had nothing to do with the boycott, of course.

Jacques Corrèze, Castres said, had been regularly informed about the negotiations with the Boycott Bureau. He formally stated that Corrèze "never participated directly or indirectly in these negotiations." A moment later, probably understanding that he had gone too far, he added, "Mr. Corrèze might have participated at certain meetings concerning the boycott as an observer, being chairman of Helena Rubinstein."

Colonel Recordon, who was conducting the interrogation, showed Castres Saint-Martin a brochure found in L'Oréal's files entitled "The General Principles of Israel's Boycott." Several phrases in this document had been underlined. No, Castres said, he hadn't seen that document, he had no idea from whom it came, and he didn't know who had brought it to L'Oréal.

Colonel Recordon wasn't very happy with Castres Saint-Martin's answers about the boycott. On his insistence, Castres returned the same afternoon and brought him a copy of his letter of February 1 to Zouheir Akil. That was the document in which L'Oréal had bent over backward to assure the boycott master that his orders had been carried out to the letter.

On June 13, Judge Getti interrogated Michel Pietrini, Paravision's president, who was already leaving the company to become president of Lanvin perfumes.

"François Dalle," Pietrini testified, "told me that only at the end of January 1989 had he found out that Jean Frydman was not a resident of Canada but of Israel. . . . Mr. Dalle committed a blunder [as far as the boycott was concerned], but he was afraid that the Israeli address of Jean Frydman might affect the cancellation of L'Oréal's boycott. I think that he also wanted to protect Mr. Owen-Jones, but he had other means to do so, and didn't need the resignation of Jean Frydman. As for the means we could have employed, we could have called a shareholders' general assembly and dismissed Mr. Frydman."

This argument was, of course, senseless. If Frydman's dismissal had been brought before a public assembly, he or somebody else on his behalf would have asked for an explanation. Frydman would never have passively accepted being kicked out of his own company.

Pietrini claimed that during his confrontation with Jean Frydman on June 22, 1989, Frydman had been the one who brought up Corrèze's name. But Jean Frydman and the two witnesses to the conversation, Catherine Morisse and Michael Stevens, stated in their testimonies that Pietrini had been the first to mention Corrèze as the man responsible for Frydman's resignation. After all, at the time Frydman had no idea who Jacques Corrèze was. And Pietrini's version didn't hold water for another reason: In June 1989 Frydman couldn't possibly have guessed that

Corrèze's name would surface in L'Oréal's notes taken at the secret meetings concerning the boycott. These notes were discovered in L'Oréal's archives only two years later.

On June 19, 1991, it was the turn of Marc Ladreit de Lacharrière, L'Oréal's vice president. In Getti's office at the Palais de Justice he admitted that at the meeting of the strategic committee on April 4, 1989, he had been asked by François Dalle to list the questions posed by the Arab Boycott Bureau to L'Oréal.

He also admitted having questioned Jean Frydman for a half hour, but he didn't remember if he had asked Frydman about his company's activities in Israel; he didn't remember Frydman's answers either. Lacharrière also admitted that the questions he had asked Frydman were inspired by the brochure titled "General Principles of Israel's Boycott." That was the same brochure that Castres Saint-Martin had sworn, a few days before, that he had never seen.

Ladreit de Lacharrière also disclosed a fact crucial for the understanding of the strange strategic committee meeting of April 4, 1989, and its consequences: Abdel Bari, the Egyptian go-between, had come to Paris at the end of March. On March 31, 1989, he had secretly met with Ladreit de Lacharrière, Gérard Sanchez, and Jacques Corrèze.

With this revelation the time sequence made perfect sense. On March 31 Abdel Bari came to Paris and secretly met with several L'Oréal officials, including Corrèze. On April 4, at the strategic committee meeting, Frydman was asked to resign. His phony resignation letter was backdated to March 30, so L'Oréal and Abdel Bari could testify that when they had met, Frydman had already resigned.

This portion of Lacharrière's testimony corroborated

other evidence Getti had obtained during the raid on the Centre Eugène Schueller. Getti said, "I found in the agenda of Saint-Martin, or somebody else, that a short while before the ouster of Jean Frydman, there was a meeting with the participation of Corrèze and some Arab League representatives in Paris. So one could assume that the name of Frydman might have been mentioned and Corrèze . . . had later said to Pietrini or Saint-Martin: 'Careful, we might have a problem with Frydman.' Perhaps that was how Corrèze had played a role in this affair, but Corrèze never admitted it. And nobody else will."

An honest man, Lacharrière admitted in his testimony that Abdel Bari was in charge of negotiating the "honorariums" to boycott officials and "important personalities" in exchange for closing L'Oréal's file. He also admitted that Corrèze had been kept current on the negotiations and had participated in many meetings with Abdel Bari. Lacharrière admitted having met Abdel Bari in March and then in May of 1989, with the intention of lowering the amount of the payoffs.

Like Pietrini, Lacharrière criticized Dalle's initiatives to make Frydman resign. "François Dalle showed excessive caution which was not justified, considering Damascus's demands. . . . I believe François Dalle asked Jean Frydman to resign before April 4. Jean-Pierre Meyers or Mr. Dalle told me he had even agreed to resign."

Lacharrière also admitted that Corrèze "was not disinterested in the situation of Helena Rubinstein Israel vis-à-vis the boycott problems." But he stressed again that, as far as he knew, "Corrèze did not intervene in Jean Frydman's ouster."

Finally, Lacharrière described the Boycott Bureau's stringent conditions for the lifting of the boycott, as reported by Claude de Kemoularia—buying up Helena Rubinstein throughout the world, stopping production in Israel, changing the Israeli company's name, answering all the questions about the relations between L'Oréal and Israel. He qualified these conditions as "double blackmail" and frankly admitted, "If we agreed to this blackmail, there would be no more boycott."

The same day, June 19, 1991, Getti interrogated the key character in the affair: François Dalle.

"I met Jean Frydman by chance in Marbella during the weekend of March 30, 1989. He told me then that he wanted to become a resident of France. I was surprised because I had always thought he was a resident of Canada. He explained to me that he was a resident of Israel, but he wanted to establish his residence in France because of his family."

Dalle testified that he then told Frydman that L'Oréal was in the middle of a process of getting out of the boycott, and "the Damascus people" might make the connection between Helena Rubinstein and Paravision.

Frydman had asked, according to Dalle, "What can I do for you?" and without waiting for Dalle's answer he had offered to resign.

Dalle added: "If the Arab League . . . had demanded of us that Jean Frydman resign, I would never have agreed." He admitted he had made a mistake by not holding the board meeting of March 30, 1989, "but it is very common in large companies that these meetings are held only on paper."

He described the strategic committee meeting at which he had asked Lacharrière to tell Frydman how the boycott functioned. "It was done very quickly," he said, "only a few minutes." (He could not know that Lacharrière had said Frydman's questioning had lasted a half hour.) On the other hand, he qualified Jean Frydman's description of the same meeting as "a detective novel," meaning it was totally invented.

That very morning, the accusations of Klarsfeld against Corrèze had been published. Dalle tried to minimize the role of Corrèze at L'Oréal. "We are in the domain of sheer madness," he said of Jean Frydman's declarations. "Jacques Corrèze didn't know Jean Frydman or Paravision; all this is a detective novel. It is normal that Corrèze would know about the Helena Rubinstein boycott, he was its chairman. But his influence in L'Oréal was practically zero. . . .

"In New York he had been a real pioneer. But he wasn't a manager; he wasn't good either at marketing or at publicity. Still, I left him with Cosmair because he had contributed a lot to that company. . . . Because of his relations with Madame Helena Rubinstein he succeeded in buying Helena Rubinstein Spain. . . . But to claim that Corrèze could have played a role in Jean Frydman's ouster is like declaring that there is no boss at L'Oréal.

"It is true that I hired Jacques Corrèze although he had been condemned twice . . . but he had just been released from jail. I don't regret having hired him, he gave me full satisfaction. Besides, I shall not take lessons in patriotism from anybody!"

Dalle again qualified as "sheer madness" Frydman's assessment that Paravision assets were worth 2.5–3 billion francs ($400–$475 million). He added that L'Oréal had decided to buy Frydman's stock "neither because of Corrèze nor because of the boycott, but because with Frydman our life had become impossible."

He bitterly complained against the press campaign triggered by Frydman. "We never believed Frydman would launch such a campaign. . . . The wrong that was done, to me and to the company, is considerable."

In the following weeks Getti completed his interrogations. Michael Stevens, a Paravision board member and chairman of Paravision U.K., supported most of Jean Frydman's accusations.

Jean Lévy, a former director general of Cosmair, testified about the presence of other collaborators, members of the notorious Milice, and other French Nazis inside L'Oréal. "Everybody inside the company knew that L'Oréal's Spanish agency was headed by the Deloncle family and that certain persons had found refuge in South and North America."

Jean Frydman was recalled twice to clarify certain points and answer some of the accusations by L'Oréal executives.

Daniela Frydman, Jean's wife, testified about the Marbella dinner with François and Geneviève Dalle. The resignation of her husband "was never mentioned during the dinner or at any other moment," she stated.

Catherine Morisse also returned to testify. She had been deeply hurt by the efforts of several L'Oréal people to discredit her, to the point of alleging she was the illegitimate daughter of Jean Frydman.

By the early fall of 1991, Judge Getti had completed his interrogations. He had read all the relevant documents and carried out another raid on the Clavier law firm. He also had requested supplementary information from L'Oréal.

As for the boycott affair, Getti had uncovered the strange complicity between L'Oréal and the ministries of foreign affairs and trade. In L'Oréal's files he found three letters written by Marc Ladreit de Lacharrière, with the approval of Ambassador de Kemoularia.

Two of the letters expressed the deep thanks of L'Oréal to the French diplomats in Damascus who had helped Kemoularia in his negotiations with the Boycott Bureau. The canceling of the boycott, Lacharrière wrote to Ambassador Grenier and to the commercial attaché Riva-Roveda, "wouldn't have been achieved without the valuable and efficient help you gave us, nor without the support and the advice of the French embassy in Syria."

A third letter was sent to the minister of foreign trade, Mr. Jean-Marie Rausch. Lacharrière effusively thanked his ministry for its help, "especially for the attention given to our affair by Mr. Olivier Louis, the commercial adviser in charge of the Third Subdirectorate."

"This affair was astounding for many reasons," Judge Getti said later, "but mostly because of the personality of its main characters. François Dalle, an extraordinary man, a great industry builder, the man who made L'Oréal into one of the most successful companies of the French economy. And Jean Frydman, a man who had an amazing life story, in France and Israel. His experience during the war is astonishing, and then, forty years later, his old enemies emerge again from the past."

Getti was deeply impressed by the dramatic clash of these two men, both larger than life. Which of the two was telling the truth?

"There could be two different interpretations of this case. Dalle says, 'Jean Frydman had agreed, we met in Marbella, and the bogus board meeting was only putting our agreement on paper.' And Jean Frydman says, 'No, no, I never agreed, this was done behind my back because of my Jewish and Israeli origins.'

"You see, we have two versions that confront each other. Dalle and his lawyers say, 'If we really wanted to remove Jean Frydman, we would have used other legal methods. . . . Board members can be evicted without any special reason . . . without explanation, so why do we need a false resignation? Why should we hold a phony board meeting if Jean Frydman hadn't agreed? Therefore it is clear that he did agree.'

"To those arguments I responded, 'You know, everybody can make mistakes or act foolishly. Perhaps you thought nobody would discover anything until L'Oréal was definitely cleared of the boycott. Then you would have reinstated Jean Frydman by another board meeting, again a phony one, and the affair would be over, Jean Frydman would be back in his position, and nothing would show.

"You see, there could have been two phony board meetings without him knowing it. If one assumes Frydman didn't know about the first meeting, it's very possible that he wouldn't have known about the second as well. He would have been reinstated, and nobody would ever have known.

"But Jean Frydman found out."

Getti had many doubts about what had really been said during the strategic committee meeting on April 4, 1989. Had Lacharrière questioned Frydman about his business in Israel? Had Dalle asked Frydman to resign? Had Frydman refused?

"It was a total misunderstanding," Getti said, laughing. "There is this one man who doesn't want to say what he thinks, and the other who doesn't want to believe what he hears. . . . I don't read hearts and minds, I can base my judgment only on material proofs, so I interpreted them my way, and I drew my conclusions."

He had to make up his mind. Were Frydman's charges serious? Did they justify an indictment?

"The two versions were possible," Getti recalled. "I had to choose one of them.

"I chose the Frydman version."

On October 22, 1991, Judge Getti indicted Michel Pietrini "for forgery, use of forgery, and racial discrimination."

On November 19, on identical charges, he indicted François Dalle.

12

The indictments of François Dalle and Michel Pietrini made the front pages of the French papers and were extensively reported in the foreign media. It was not every day that a businessman of Dalle's stature was indicted. And this definitely was the first time that one had been charged with breaking the antiboycott laws.

In his press interviews, Dalle was bitter and dejected. The seventy-three-year-old man had made a wonderful career and won the gratitude of his nation, the respect and the admiration of his peers. Now he was approaching the end of the road. But instead of a golden retirement he was probably going to be dragged to court in a messy trial. This was certainly not the way for an empire builder to exit the stage.

Following the fraud judgment against Mayoux and the Corrèze scandal, Dalle's indictment was the third consecutive victory for the Frydman brothers, and the most important one. A well-known judge whose integrity and competence nobody contested had accepted Jean Frydman's version of the facts. It proved that the accusations against L'Oréal were not baseless; the company had apparently yielded to the Arab boycott.

Until recently the general feeling in Paris had been that the L'Oréal affair was really a money grab. Many, including prominent Jews, had sincerely believed that the Frydmans were accusing L'Oréal of boycott, racism, and Nazi connections only to embarrass the firm and thereby obtain a better financial settlement. Now they had to admit, albeit grudgingly, that the Frydmans' campaign was being waged on questions of principle.

Following the revelations about L'Oréal, several groups, most of them Jewish, combined to file class action against L'Oréal for violating the boycott laws. The groups included the CRIF, the official Jewish community organization, the Chamber of Commerce France–Israel, and the David association. A crusading association of lawyers, Avocats Sans Frontières—Lawyers Without Borders— also joined the roll of plaintiffs.

Their initiative stemmed from the fact that the Frydman brothers could sue L'Oréal for personal discrimination, but being private persons they had no legal standing in a suit against L'Oréal for breaking the antiboycott laws. This kind of charge could be pressed either by the state prosecutors or by recognized associations. The man who put together the joint Jewish front was Jean Kahn, the president of the French Jewish community. Another active militant in this initiative was a young lawyer, William Goldnadel, the president of Avocats Sans Frontières.

The president of the Chamber of Commerce France–Israel, Lionel Stoleru, hesitated for a long time before joining the effort. Some members of the Chamber of Commerce board thought he wavered because L'Oréal had been one of the founding members of his organization. He tried to find a way out of his dilemma by proposing to his board that they first conduct a "hearing" of the L'Oréal lawyers to find out if there really were grounds for the accusations.

Maurice Kahan, an influential member of the board, firmly objected to the idea and said he would vote against it. For years Kahan had been supporting Serge Klarsfeld's projects. He was the one who had investigated Corrèze and the boycott, and even had tried to speak to Corrèze in his apartment. The final push that motivated Stoleru to join the other Jewish organizations was a fax from Jean Kahn. "If you don't join us, we'll do it without you," Kahn's message said in essence. It worked.

L'Oréal meanwhile was disconcerted by the behavior of the media. It had a well-staffed communications and public relations department, headed by a vice president. It employed the services of France's largest advertising and public relations firm, Publicis. L'Oréal was the largest advertiser in France, holding a 40-percent share of the spending throughout the nation. And yet its influence over the media in its conflict with the Frydman brothers seemed to be negligible.

A smart, aggressive press campaign was waged against the cosmetics company, fueled by zesty revelations and sensational documents from L'Oréal's boycott files. L'Oréal's bosses were convinced that Jean Frydman was constantly supplying facts and documents to the press. How else, they thought, could documents seized in our vaults by the gendarmerie and handed to the Frydmans' lawyers find their way to the newspapers?

L'Oréal didn't know how to deal with the revelations in the press. Like a clumsy pachyderm the huge company moved too slowly, unable to match the determination and agility of its small opponents.

"I was sometimes embarrassed," Getti said later, "because Jean Frydman talked [to the press] too much . . . but he knows how to do it. He is a man of the media. I believe this was Frydman's main advantage in this affair vis-à-vis Dalle and L'Oréal. I was surprised by L'Oréal's inability to work with the media in this affair. They have a press service at L'Oréal, but Frydman, all alone, was a hundred times better. His offensive in the media drove Dalle to make a mistake. He said, 'Frydman is using the Holocaust to make money.' I believe Dalle had an unfortunate slip of the tongue that certainly exceeded his thoughts, for I am convinced that Dalle is not an anti-Semite."

L'Oréal was well aware of its disadvantage. On November 29, 1991, the company finally decided to counterattack, and released a statement to the press.

Implicated by the media, following the declarations of Mr. Frydman concerning his conflict with Paravision, L'Oréal has decided to restore the truth of the matter.

In early 1982, the prestigious cosmetics company Helena Rubinstein was in trouble. Its owners decided to sell some far-away subsidiaries in order to better concentrate on the large European markets.

That's how in 1983 L'Oréal bought the subsidiaries in Latin America and Japan in order to strengthen its own business in these countries.

But Helena Rubinstein had been boycotted for a long time by the Arab League. Automatically, the Arab League decided to boycott L'Oréal. For no reason, as L'Oréal, neither in its activity nor in its organization, offered a real motive for boycott.

L'Oréal, therefore, had to defend itself. . . . It received a questionnaire [from the Boycott Bureau]. . . .

It answered it in order to try to stop the process, but with the firm intention not to yield on the main issues, according to the instructions of its president at the time, Mr. Charles Zwiak.

More letters [from the Boycott Bureau] followed. There was no other choice but to reply with ruses. By asking for further delays, by skirting the important questions. L'Oréal even . . . pretended to give satisfaction to the Damascus bureau, while really trying not to change its traditional commercial strategy.

But the executives of the Arab League quickly understood that . . . [and] in early 1988 the Damascus bureau called all the Arab League nations to boycott all of L'Oréal's business.

L'Oréal therefore "changed tactics" and turned for help to Ambassador Claude de Kemoularia, asking him to make the Damascus bureau understand that there was no reason to keep L'Oréal on the blacklist. After two trips by Kemoularia to Damascus, "it became clear" that the company had been boycotted "wrongly."

Once again, for the sake of convincing the Damascus executives, L'Oréal presented . . . arrangements achieved in the past, in full agreement with its Israeli partners and for wholly technical reasons—as concessions. . . .

L'Oréal is basically hostile to the very principle of the boycott. . . . It never strayed from the laws in force. . . . L'Oréal never harmed the interests of its Israeli partners.

This statement was signed by Jean-Pierre Valeriola, the director general of the public relations department of

L'Oréal. In spite of offering rather convoluted, incomplete, and not always accurate explanations, it had a good chance of making an impact on public opinion. But the release had barely reached the press agencies when a much more sensational story hit the teleprinters: reliable sources accused L'Oréal of paying bribes to Arab officials. This accusation had been made in the past, but now the allegations were supported by authentic documents from L'Oréal's archives.

L'Oréal had no choice but to release another communiqué, several hours after the first. It admitted that, yes, it had indeed paid a million dollars in "honorariums" to prominent Arabs through its Egyptian contact, Abdel Bari. The payments had been made in October 1989. L'Oréal added that the money was paid to Abdel Bari because of the "hard pressures" made against him. That meant Bari had been threatened. Abdel Bari had failed in his mission, Valeriola said, but after the boycott had been lifted he told L'Oréal: "I asked many people for help, and they believe I owe them something."

Valeriola added that the company had no idea how the money had been used. It is probable that Valeriola indeed didn't know the identities of Abdel Bari's friends. But Valeriola's colleagues at L'Oréal who had met so many times with the wily Egyptian knew perfectly well who had been paid off.

The bribes, of course, were what made the headlines. The effect on public opinion of this new admission by L'Oréal was devastating.

Yet more was to come. From the disarray at L'Oréal came a leak of explosive new information.

Maurice Szafran was the darkly handsome star reporter of the weekly newsmagazine *L'Événement du*

Jeudi. On November 25, 1991, he wrote a detailed article about L'Oréal and the boycott. All his efforts to get a comment from L'Oréal had failed. His article was almost completed when he succeeded in obtaining a last-minute interview with Pierre Castres Saint-Martin, L'Oréal's financial director. Because the magazine deadline was 4 P.M. on Tuesday the twenty-sixth, he rushed to Clichy early that morning and was shown into Castres Saint-Martin's office.

Szafran found before him "a terrified man." He quickly realized why. Castres, as financial director and the man responsible for contacts with the Boycott Bureau, had been the one who signed all the documents in the course of the negotiations. He therefore feared that he might become a scapegoat for everybody else.

Castres was ready to go very far in order to show his goodwill, and to prove that he was only a tiny cog in the huge machine. He took a paper from his files and gave it to the surprised Szafran. It was a letter to Zouheir Akil from Claude de Kemoularia, dated July 4, 1988. This letter had not been found by the gendarmes during their raid on L'Oréal.

The two-page letter strongly implicated Kemoularia. He explicitly promised the Boycott Bureau that L'Oréal would contact HR Israel and make sure that by the end of the year Helena Rubinstein stopped not only all production in the Jewish state but also all exports carrying the Helena Rubinstein name. This directly contravened the policy he had promoted in the Mideast seven years before. And it clearly violated French law.

Szafran hurried back to his office and inserted the letter in his article. But he had barely finished when he got a surprising phone call.

"Mr. X would like to speak to you, sir," a secretary said.

Mr. X* was a Jewish personage connected with L'Oréal. Szafran knew that L'Oréal was a large advertiser in his magazine, so he expected to hear something like: "Be careful. You know that L'Oréal buys a great deal of advertising in your magazine, so why don't you ask your editor his opinion before you publish this article?"

But Mr. X chose a different approach. "Dear Maurice," he said, "please be cautious. This affair is not at all good for us."

"For us? Who is 'us'?"

"Come on, you know what I mean. I spoke to Owen-Jones. They are going to invest a lot in Israel, but this is a very bad story for the Jewish community. Besides, Jean Frydman is absolutely incorrect in this affair." In other words, the L'Oréal affair might stir anti-Jewish feelings in France.

Szafran gave a noncommittal answer and hung up. He had no doubt that Mr. X had called him because of his interview with Castres Saint-Martin. Szafran had expected to encounter pressure, but not of the sort targeting his Jewish origins. He later realized that in many cases L'Oréal used Jews—like Jean-Pierre Meyers, the lawyer Jean Veil, or Mr. X—to speak to other Jews.

The article was published, unchanged, on Thursday, November 28, 1991. It described the strange role of Kemoularia, who ten years before had promoted the antiboycott law but then had proceeded to savage it. He probably had been paid a fortune by L'Oréal for his efforts. Szafran also mentioned the zealous cooperation of the French em-

---

* The name and the public/professional positions of Mr. X are known to the author, but withheld by agreement with Mr. Szafran.

bassy in Damascus with the former U.N. ambassador, a man known to be a personal friend of President Mitterrand.

A few days after the article in *L'Événement du Jeudi* was published, Jean Frydman got a telephone call from the Élysée Palace. President Mitterrand's adviser Charles Salzmann was on the line.

"I have to see you, Jean," he said. "You're coming too close."

13

"Charles Salzmann is secrecy incarnated," says Hubert Védrine, the chief of staff of the Palais de l'Élysée under President Mitterrand.

"He is a man of mystery," agrees Jacques Attali, another Mitterrand adviser. "Officially, he was a technical adviser to the president, in charge of public opinion polls. I knew him in that function. But I believe that the polls were only a front, and he had other, very secret functions for the president. Perhaps you should look into his past to find the key to this mystery."

Salzmann's past reveals only hints about his real activities. A tall, bony man in his sixties, an admirer of Israel, he held a degree in aeronautical engineering from the University of Paris and a master's from Columbia University in New York. He had been president of the French Center for Operational [military] Research for ten years. For two years he had worked at the Institute for Higher Studies on National Defense. In 1981, with Mitterrand's election, he had been appointed "technical adviser" to the president. Nothing in his past qualified him for evaluating public opinion polls.

According to certain sources he accompanied François Mitterrand on his trips to the Soviet Union during the eighties and helped him with his talks because of his fluency in Russian. Mitterrand also put him in charge of discreet contacts with the Soviets and later with the new Russian government.

Other sources claim that Salzmann was President Mitterrand's assistant for delicate matters requiring a heavy veil of secrecy. By 1989 Salzmann had officially left the president's service and had been appointed chairman of the board of the French company that dug and managed the tunnel under Mont Blanc. Still, he kept an office at the Élysée Palace and continued regularly meeting with the president.

Salzmann also had been a member of the secret committee formed in 1981 that prepared and executed Mitterrand's new antiboycott strategy. "I am very proud," he said, "that between the years 1981 and 1983 I could do something that served the interests of both France and Israel."

Salzmann knew Jean Frydman well. It was to him that Jean Frydman had come two years before, when he was illegally evicted from Paravision. Salzmann had introduced Frydman to the young Mark Boudier, who harshly condemned L'Oréal's compliance with the boycott.

Salzmann now met Frydman again at the presidential palace. "Listen, Jean," he said, "this story has gone too far. We don't want to see Kemoularia coming out of the judge's office in handcuffs." It was clear to Frydman that Salzmann was speaking for the president, although he didn't mention him by name.

He then asked Jean Frydman to drop the charges against L'Oréal.

Frydman was stunned. The president of France was intervening for L'Oréal in a legal matter? He had not expected such a demand, and at first he could see no reason for it.

Salzmann offered Frydman a deal. If he dropped his charges against L'Oréal, a board of inquiry would be established. This board would be sponsored by the main Jewish organizations of France. They too would drop their charges against L'Oréal. The board would be headed by Professor Bismuth, a Jew as well, who was considered the supreme authority on the boycott in France. Bismuth, it should be recalled, had also been a member of the antiboycott committee in 1981.

The board would review the documents and find out if L'Oréal had indeed violated French laws. It would publish its findings, and L'Oréal would cooperate with the inquiry. If any infraction was detected, the Élysée would act to reinforce the antiboycott legislation.

Frydman was deeply impressed by the fact that the presidency had decided to intervene in the affair. He promised Salzmann an answer and left his office.

What was behind Salzmann's proposal? There was no doubt that he did not act on his own initiative. In a conversation with a friend, Salzmann vigorously denied that President Mitterrand had ever mentioned L'Oréal in his presence. But after repeated questions, he finally admitted that at least once, during a meeting at the Élysée Palace, Mitterrand had angrily shown him the newspapers and asked, "What does your friend Jean Frydman want with this L'Oréal story?"

Hubert Védrine, chief of staff and the closest man to the president, also told Salzmann several times that the L'Oréal affair was very unpleasant. He didn't want the affair discussed in the press, since the newspapers published "all kinds of things."

"You're telling me a strange story," Salzmann's friend remarked. "You say that the president of France reads the papers and finds out that one of the largest companies of France, which is owned and managed by two of Mitterrand's closest friends, Dalle and Bettencourt, is violating the law. Not any law, but a law promulgated by the president and identified with him. And what does the president do? He doesn't try to enforce the law. He doesn't order an investigation of L'Oréal. He blames the man who fights against this violation. Don't you find this odd?"

The president was motivated by a single concern, Salzmann answered stiffly. All that mattered for him was the national interest of France.

As for Hubert Védrine, one of the reasons he gave for his decision to get actively involved in the affair was the fact that he "had lots of friends at L'Oréal at the management level." Still, Védrine added, "my involvement started when Salzmann came to see me and said, 'This L'Oréal affair is very embarrassing. It is creating the impression that the Élysée isn't fighting the boycott as strongly as it should.' "

"Why have you come to see me?" Vedrine asked.

"I would like you to host a meeting about the boycott. Perhaps we should call several people, like Jean Kahn, Professor Bismuth, and others, and investigate if L'Oréal has indeed yielded to the boycott."

"If I understand you correctly," Védrine said, "you want me to give this investigation my moral and administrative authority. You want me, if needed, to call cabinet ministers and government officials and tell them that the presidency of the republic is behind this investigation."

"Precisely," Salzmann said.

"But I cannot do this on my own. I'll have to ask the president."

"Don't bother," Salzmann said. "I'm having dinner with him tonight. I'll talk to him."

The next morning Salzmann was back. "I spoke to the president. He agrees."

In the following days Védrine and Salzmann intervened vigorously in the affair. Salzmann called Jean Kahn, the president of the Jewish community in France. Kahn, a strong, independent Alsatian from the city of Strasbourg, enjoyed an unprecedented authority as the leader of France's Jews. A silver-haired, handsome man known for his moral courage, Jean Kahn knew Frydman well but was not a close friend. Nobody could suspect Kahn of any financial motivation for pressing charges against L'Oréal, or for wanting to help Frydman in his crusade. Besides, Kahn had a good working relationship with President Mitterrand.

Salzmann met with Kahn several times, in Kahn's office and at the Élysée Palace. Hubert Védrine also contacted Kahn, and the two men met at Védrine's office at the Élysée. Theo Klein, a prominent lawyer and a former president of the Jewish community, also met Védrine.

The chief of staff seemed anxious to resolve the L'Oréal affair the way Salzmann had suggested to Jean Frydman. In these conversations the creation of the Bismuth board of inquiry was discussed in detail. Clearly Védrine was acting not only because of his personal sympathy to some "good friends" at L'Oréal but because of the president's instructions. It seemed that the presidency was ready to go very far in order to stop the legal proceedings against L'Oréal.

Jean Kahn and Jean Frydman finally got together. Kahn suggested that both parties—Frydman and the Jewish organizations—agree to the Élysée request and drop the charges against L'Oréal on two conditions:

One, a public condemnation of the boycott by the president, who would launch an initiative for uniform European legislation against the boycott. He could do that by securing the support of his partners in the European Community.

Two, the establishment of a board of inquiry headed by Professor Bismuth.

Jean Frydman returned to Charles Salzmann. In a short memorandum he had put the two conditions in writing. They both started with the words: "The president undertakes to . . ."

Salzmann read the memorandum. "Give me fifteen minutes," he said to Frydman and left the office. Frydman realized he had gone to see the president.

Soon after, Salzmann was back. "It's okay," he said.

The Frydman brothers were impressed both by the president's intervention and by his promises. They felt they couldn't pursue their struggle against his request. Frydman had known Mitterrand since 1945, and had met with him before and after his election. He had been his guest for lunch at the Élysée. He trusted him as a man of his word, and as a friend of Israel. He was ready to drop the charges.

The organizations that had pressed charges reacted in the same way. But there was one dissenter: Avocats Sans Frontières. William Goldnadel was deeply involved in the struggle and wanted to fight to the end.

When he had first learned of the affair, Goldnadel had been suspicious of the Frydman brothers. He felt they were businessmen pursuing their private interests. Then he had heard that one of their lawyers was former foreign minister Michel Jobert and became even more distrustful.

"A good Jew can't hire Jobert as a lawyer," he thought. "Something is wrong here." Besides, some Jewish businessmen had spoken to him of the Frydmans in very harsh terms. "I hate when a Jew who is involved in some commercial conflict says: 'I was wronged because I'm Jewish.'"

Once he probed the core of the matter, however, Goldnadel's attitude changed completely, and he became convinced of the brothers' sincerity. He wholeheartedly embraced their cause and gladly filed charges against L'Oréal.

He soon felt an ill wind blowing from the presidential palace. When he had filed the suit against L'Oréal, he had been warned by several judges not to become involved. "Careful, you don't know what you're doing. This is one of the most explosive cases in France, because the Élysée Palace is constantly intervening!" He recalls that even Judge Getti had admonished him to be cautious. "You don't know where you're stepping, Counselor," Getti purportedly said to him.

Indeed, a full six months had passed since he filed charges, and a *juge d'instruction* still hadn't been appointed to investigate his case. (As this lawsuit was separate from the Frydmans', Judge Getti could not investigate it.) Clearly, the public prosecutor's office was intentionally slowing down the process.

In early December, Jean Frydman came to see Goldnadel and, telling him about the agreement with the Élysée, asked him to drop the charges against L'Oréal. At first Goldnadel refused. He did not share Frydman's high opinion of the president. "The Frydman brothers are naive in a way," he said later. "They belong to a generation that believes a left-wing president is on the side of the Jews, a right-wing one against them. They sincerely believed Mitterrand was a friend of the Jewish people. I didn't."

He finally agreed to drop the charges, mostly because he feared that the suit would be buried for years in the judicial maze and never come to trial. But when he gave up, he firmly warned Jean and David Frydman, "You're making a mistake. Mark my words!"

Finally, Jean Frydman came to Judge Getti's office. "I have been approached by the Élysée Palace," he said, "to consider dropping the charges."

On December 13, 1991, Judge Getti invited Frydman, Dalle, and their lawyers to his office at the Palais de Justice. It was a cold night, with icy gusts rising from the river and sweeping the streets of the Île de la Cité. An atmosphere of tension and suspicion reigned in Judge Getti's office.

Getti said, "I have completed my investigation. Here is the case, and here is what I think. I intend to refer this case to the court, because I believe it contains sufficient elements for a ruling. The court will decide if L'Oréal has broken the law. If it says yes, it will pronounce a sentence. If not, it will be an acquittal." Getti then expressed his personal conclusion. "I have found in this affair a case of racial discrimination in the framework of economic activity."

These words were directed at Dalle and his lawyers. Getti had just told them that he had found enough grounds to charge L'Oréal with breaking the law. They exchanged glances. They might have a long trial ahead, which could be a nightmare for Dalle and for L'Oréal.

The judge paused. "Now," he said, "if Mr. Frydman believes, at the end of the investigation, that this discrimination results from a wrong understanding of the acts of Mr. Dalle, or a wrong interpretation of the statements made by Mr. Dalle, and if anybody in this case is ready to suggest a way to put an end to this discrimination, I am ready to listen."

There was a moment of astounded silence. Then Dalle's lawyers realized that the judge was offering them a way out. A trial could be avoided if a compromise was found.

When François Dalle recovered from the initial shock, he asked if he could talk with Jean Frydman alone. Getti turned to the lawyers, who hastily agreed. "We all left the room," Getti recalled later, "and they remained alone for quite a while."

When the judge and the lawyers came back into the office, the two men announced that they had reached an agreement. François Dalle would write a letter of apology to Frydman, who would accept it and drop the charges, on the premise that the perception of racial discrimination was the result of a misapprehension.

Dalle also promised Frydman that the various complaints L'Oréal had filed against him and his brother in retaliation would be dropped as well.

On December 19, 1991, François Dalle wrote to Frydman:

Monsieur,

For many months we have found ourselves confronted in a painful conflict on civil and penal grounds.

In fact, our conflicts are based on a dramatic misunderstanding of the circumstances in which you have been driven to leave the Paravision company.

I understand that this misunderstanding has hurt you cruelly, and I feel sincere regrets for this situation, but you have acknowledged that at no moment could I

have participated in an act that would have been motivated by discrimination, which always has disgusted
me.

You must admit as well that the initiatives and the
accusations expressed against me during the proceedings, especially the criminal charges, were unjust and
have painfully affected me.

Therefore we agreed before *Monsieur le Juge
d'Instruction* that reason and wisdom ordered us to put
an end to our destructive conflicts as soon as possible.

I recognize willingly that certain expressions I had
used in private and which the press had published
were equally injurious and unjust, and I confirm that
the resolution of our conflict does not include any financial counterpart.

As we have succeeded in dispelling these misun-
derstandings, I undertake to do all in my power to put
an end to the rumors concerning you, and I count on
you to do the same.

(*signed*) François Dalle.

On December 20, 1991, Jean Frydman replied:

Monsieur,

I have received your letter, whose terms reflect exactly our conversation in the presence of Monsieur
Getti on December 13.

Please accept, Monsieur, my best regards,

(*signed*) Jean Frydman.

The closing of Frydman's letter was not as cordial
as direct translation implies. Of the formulas used by
the French in personal correspondence, it was in fact the
coolest—and carefully judged.

In a letter to Getti, Jean Frydman confirmed he was dropping the charges against Dalle and thanked him for his investigation.

Almost a year later, Judge Getti officially announced the dismissal of the case. L'Oréal immediately declared that the dismissal proved the full innocence of its executives—which was, of course, not so.

There could be no doubt that without the courage and determination of Judge Getti, the affair might have died on December 17, 1990, when Jean Frydman filed his charges against L'Oréal. Years later Getti reflected on the clash between Frydman and L'Oréal. When asked why L'Oréal didn't make an effort to reach a compromise with Jean Frydman and end the affair quietly before it exploded, he responded:

"I've asked myself this question. They were powerful. And when you are too powerful you become stupid because you are too confident. I'd define their behavior as 'the stupidity of the mighty.'

"They thought: 'We are L'Oréal, we are strong. I am François Dalle, I am powerful, et cetera. . . . Frydman is small, we'll crush him, and the affair will be over.' But Frydman didn't let them scare him. It was David and Goliath.

"For me," Judge Getti concluded, "this was the most fascinating affair of my career."

But even though Jean-Pierre Getti's part in the drama had ended, the L'Oréal affair was far from over.

14

President Mitterrand didn't keep his word.

He mentioned the boycott in a speech at a European conference in Lisbon, but that was the end of his initiative. European antiboycott legislation was not modified.

In early 1993 a meeting was convened by Hubert Védrine in his Palais de l'Élysée office. The participants were Charles Salzmann, Jean Kahn, Professor Bismuth, and a few senior officials. They resolved to carry out an inquiry to establish whether L'Oréal had submitted to the Arab boycott. The inquiry would be entrusted to Professor Bismuth, with the full cooperation of the various branches of government. L'Oréal agreed to pay Bismuth's honorarium through an intermediary law firm. Védrine and Salzmann promised the full help of the Élysée.

The Bismuth inquiry soon ran into difficulties. The frustrated professor bitterly complained to the Jewish community president, Jean Kahn, that he was running into brick walls and was being refused the assistance of various administrative branches, especially the Ministry of Foreign Trade. Kahn immediately alerted Charles Salzmann. When President Mitterrand heard about this sabotage of Bismuth's work, Salzmann reported, he flew into "a terrible rage." But he didn't take any action. Even the Jewish minister of foreign trade, Dominique Strauss-Kahn, failed to get his subordinates to open their files for Bismuth.

In an interview Védrine recalled that he tried at least twice to make the various ministries cooperate with Bismuth, with no success. He joined forces with Strauss-Kahn, but failed, like him, to obtain access to the necessary documents for Bismuth. The officials doggedly cited various laws and regulations that allegedly prohibited outsiders any access to the files.

Then, on April 27, 1993, the forty-seven-year-old Bismuth suddenly died. The untimely passing of this brilliant scholar put an abrupt end to the Élysée's involvement in the boycott investigation. The presidential palace could have approached another expert to pursue Bismuth's research, but they didn't do so. The fact is, Bismuth's death was very convenient for many people. It cut short a delicate investigation that could rock France's political boat once again.

On May 7, ten days after Bismuth's death, one of L'Oréal's lawyers had a conversation with Bernard Jouanneau, Jean and David Frydman's attorney. He discreetly offered him a deal: the Frydman brothers would be paid the amount they asked for their shares at Paravision in exchange for their silence on the boycott affair. Jouanneau indignantly refused. He afterward called David Frydman and asked if he should have consulted him first. "If you were here now, I would have hugged you!" David Frydman answered, deeply moved.

Three days later, he dispatched personal letters to Charles Salzmann, President Mitterrand's adviser, and Jean Kahn, the president of the Jewish community, in which he related the incident—not omitting to name the lawyer who had made the offer to Jouanneau.

Now that Bismuth was dead, L'Oréal might have hoped that the report on the boycott would not be written. But the organizations that had joined in supporting Bismuth's mission didn't give up. On their own, they sponsored another famous law professor, David Ruzie, to carry out the investigation. L'Oréal vehemently objected to Ruzie's appointment, claiming that he wasn't objective. According to them, he was both the adviser of David, one of the sponsoring groups, and an associate of William Goldnadel. Both assertions were false.

Ruzie's report was completed on November 2, 1993, and it was devastating for L'Oréal. It stated that the company had clearly violated the French antiboycott laws. "From documents to which the undersigned had access, it was confirmed that L'Oréal, through some of its subsidiaries, gave boycott guarantees against Israel long before the . . . closing of Helena Rubinstein in Israel in 1988."

Ruzie had not a good word for L'Oréal. He quoted letters by Chimex, a L'Oréal subsidiary, and Gesparal, its holding company, in which they had answered boycott questionnaires. He also scrutinized the letters exchanged between L'Oréal and the Arab Boycott Bureau in the years 1986–89 and found they expressed "L'Oréal's concern to conform to the Arab boycott rules, not only from a formal point of view but, indeed, substantially."

Professor Ruzie also hinted that something was wrong with L'Oréal's claim that the HR Israel production line had been closed for "efficiency" reasons. "If it is true that the closing of the HR factory in Israel was planned in the framework of a reconstruction program, why did L'Oréal not say so immediately, in January 1987, but only announced it in October 1988?

"Incontestably," the report read, "the leaders of L'Oréal expressed the clear intention of following the rules of the boycott which the French legislation had as clearly condemned. The motive does not matter, only the intention counts. Thus, the fact that L'Oréal claims ex post facto that actually, in negotiating with the boycott authorities, it was engaged in a pretense, has no bearing on the existence of the offense. . . .

"Upon these grounds,

"The undersigned concludes that L'Oréal violated French legislation, particularly in respect of the boycott measures issued by the authorities of the Arab League."

When the report was completed L'Oréal angrily rejected it. For a while it was kept secret by the Jewish organizations, but in January 1994 it finally leaked to the press. However, most of the newspapers and TV channels didn't even mention it, and Ruzie suspected that L'Oréal had brought pressure to bear on the media.

Privately, however, L'Oréal acted in a wholly different fashion. In a telephone conversation with Jean Kahn, Lindsay Owen-Jones asked frankly, "What do you think we should do now?"

Kahn organized a secret meeting at the Paris Intercontinental Hotel. Besides Kahn and Owen-Jones the meeting was attended by top L'Oréal executives, Maurice Lévy of Publicis, and a guest of supreme importance— Uri Savir, the director general of the Israeli ministry of foreign affairs. The subject of the discussion was how

L'Oréal could make amends to Israel and wipe the slate clean.

At the meeting O.J. offered a corporate contribution to the State of Israel, which Savir rejected. "We don't want charity," he said. Instead he presented two demands. One was public recognition by L'Oréal of the responsibility of Owen-Jones's predecessors in the boycott affair as Owen-Jones himself had not been involved in that matter. Second was the establishment by L'Oréal of a plant in Israel "in its own field of activity," meaning cosmetics. At the end of the meeting it was agreed that L'Oréal would openly return to Israel to invest in the Israeli cosmetics industry and in several research projects.

Changing political tides had of course made these concessions much easier for L'Oréal to grant. The historic agreement between Israel and the PLO had been signed several months before, on September 13, 1993, on the White House lawn. Peace was coming to the Middle East, and many Arab states were willing, if not to cancel the boycott rules, at least to ignore them.

Lindsay Owen-Jones kept his promise. In May 1994 he flew to Israel with a delegation of his men and met with the top executives of Interbeauty. He announced that L'Oréal would buy 30 percent of Interbeauty for $7 million, becoming the largest shareholder in the company; it would also invest in dermatology and cosmetics research in Israeli laboratories. A few months later, L'Oréal contributed a million dollars to a traffic safety campaign in Israel.

The L'Oréal-Interbeauty deal proved that the absurd has no limits. Both L'Oréal and the Frydman brothers emerged rather battered and impoverished from the boycott scandal. L'Oréal's public image had suffered. Besides the high legal fees, Jean Frydman had lost money and clients in France. Those who really profited most from the boycott affair were the owners of Helena Rubinstein Israel. In 1989 they had been lured into closing a production line, getting in exchange cheaper products and the exclusive representation of the famous L'Oréal brands. In 1994 their stock soared as L'Oréal bought one-third of the company.

What's more, L'Oréal's lawyers were still pressing charges against the Frydman brothers.

When the agreement between François Dalle and Jean Frydman had been concluded in Judge Getti's chambers, Dalle had promised Frydman that L'Oréal would drop all the charges against the two brothers. In the following weeks, though, L'Oréal's lawyers reneged on that agreement.

On May 25, 1992, Michel Jobert, one of Frydman's lawyers, sent a personal letter to Senator André Bettencourt, L'Oréal's owner. Jobert, a former minister of foreign affairs, used to be on friendly terms with Bettencourt, but in his letter he expressed his disappointment at failing to reach Bettencourt on the telephone for several weeks. "Where are the happy times," he bitterly asked, "when neither of us had any difficulty in reaching the other?"

The letter went on: "I met attorney René Bondoux, L'Oréal's lawyer, and told him of my concern at witnessing . . . a resumption of hostilities between L'Oréal and the Frydman brothers, apparently on the initiative of L'Oréal's attorneys. I don't know if you have been informed of these developments, which seem to me quite worrying. Especially after an agreement was apparently reached in Judge Getti's chambers, following the urgent intervention of the Presidency.

"I can't measure L'Oréal's determination to try for a

settlement instead of a confrontation. On the other hand, I know the resolution of the Frydman brothers not to leave further skirmishes without riposte. . . . I fear we are moving away from an appeased climate."

The letter wasn't answered.

Both sides were soon entangled in a maze of eighteen lawsuits that might last well beyond the year 2000. Many of the Frydman cases were entrusted to Bernard Jouanneau, and some to a brilliant young lawyer, a master of prose style, Didier Scornicky.

The most important suit was the one Jean and David Frydman filed against Cosmair, L'Oréal's exclusive agent in the United States, charging Cosmair with complying with the Arab boycott. These were serious charges, considering that American antiboycott legislation was much tougher than the French. The Baxter affair was an ominous example.

In 1993 the world's largest hospital-supply company, Baxter International, admitted it had bowed to the Arab boycott. Baxter, based in Deerfield, Illinois, had been blacklisted in 1975 because it had established an Israeli subsidiary, Travenol. In 1988, yielding to Arab demands, Baxter sold Travenol to the Israeli company Teva Pharmaceuticals. Travenol was a profitable company, and Baxter's only reason for selling it was to get off the boycott list—as it shortly did. The American company then tried to build an intravenous fluids plant in Syria, in a joint venture with the Syrian army, but the plans failed.

Oddly enough, the Swiss food giant Nestlé, L'Oréal's partner, was involved in the Baxter affair as well. Three months after the Arab boycott on Baxter was lifted, Baxter signed a multimillion-dollar deal with Nestlé for the establishment of a fifty-fifty joint venture, Clintec International, to develop and market clinical nutritional products worldwide. "Nestlé," *Business Week* wrote, "which has a substantial Mideast business, did not want to alienate its Arab customers by teaming up with a blacklisted company."

The U.S. Commerce Department and Justice Department carried out a probe and established that Baxter had complied with the boycott regulations. In 1993 Baxter was sentenced to pay a fine of $6.5 million.

The Baxter affair may become a precedent for the Cosmair trial, which is pending in the United States. Some L'Oréal executives, in unofficial talks with the author of this book, estimated that $100 million is at stake in this new confrontation with Jean Frydman—and L'Oréal will be involved once again because in August 1994 it decided to buy back Cosmair from Nestlé for $1.5 billion.

L'Oréal's move coincided with the call of two New York congressmen, Charles Schumer and Jerrold Nadler, both Democrats, to boycott L'Oréal in retaliation for its having yielded to the Arab boycott of Israel. At a public meeting in New York, Nadler waved a L'Oréal hair-coloring ad featuring actress Cybill Shepherd. "We will not stand idly by," he declared, "while L'Oréal tries to put a pretty face on this immoral and illegal boycott of the nation of Israel. I call upon all Americans to renounce L'Oréal and its products."

Similar calls came from several Jewish organizations, and L'Oréal shares temporarily plunged on the stock markets. The onslaught by the American Jewish community and the American press was such that the company hastily published a statement claiming it had not yielded to the boycott.

The statement angered former New York mayor Ed Koch, who called for a boycott of L'Oréal products on WABC talk radio. Accusing it of anti-Semitism, Koch cited one of L'Oréal's letters to the Arab Boycott Bureau, in which the cosmetics company assured the boycott officials that "it had complied with all the regulations of the boycott of Israel."

In addition, Koch wrote a furious letter to Guy Peyrelongue, Cosmair's president. "What other conclusion could one come to," Koch wrote, quoting L'Oréal's letter, "after reading that as soon as L'Oréal became the owner of Helena Rubinstein 'the directors of [the HR] companies were dismissed and replaced by new directors'? Am I wrong to assume that most of the prior directors were Jewish and few if any of the directors that you appointed were Jewish? Am I wrong to assume that you did that to please the Arab League? Am I wrong to assume that when you state in the letter, 'Our company modified the company name,' that too was done to eliminate your Jewish problem?"

The fiery Koch didn't mince words. "I have no doubt that you complied [with the boycott]. Your correspondence with the Arab League reeks of your duplicitousness. I hope that every human being who uses your products will be so offended by your actions . . . and by your vacuous explanation and apology that they will continue to boycott your products."

The charges against Cosmair in New York received extensive coverage in the American press. On August 15, 1994, the Frydman brothers published a full-page ad in the *New York Times* in which they reproduced documents proving L'Oréal had complied with the boycott rules. But when asked, they objected to any boycott of L'Oréal products. Jean said, "I am not fighting a company or its products, I am fighting the men who own it. L'Oréal's products are not Nazi products. I have nothing against L'Oréal the fine cosmetics company. My struggle is against the parallel L'Oréal, the one that became a safe haven for Nazi criminals and yielded to the boycott."

The Frydman brothers were represented in pretrial motions by the noted New York lawyer Stanley Arkin. For a time former presidential candidate Ed Muskie also was involved in the Frydmans' case. The evidence against Cosmair was also submitted to Eloise Gore, the vice president's sister, who heads the Office of Antiboycott Compliance of the U.S. Department of Commerce.

The boycott scandal had now crossed the Atlantic Ocean. The next battle in the war between the Frydman brothers and L'Oréal was going to be waged in America.

Yet, when looking back, Jean Frydman felt that he had made a mistake in accepting the Élysée offer and dropping the charges against L'Oréal. He felt he should have fought to the end. When he and David later met William Goldnadel, they told him grimly: "You were right!"

Jean and David Frydman could find partial consolation in an official letter they received on November 10, 1994.

"A number of Arab countries," the letter said, "have recently taken the wise decision to radically loosen the economic boycott that they had imposed upon our country. . . . The Arab boycott has still to dissipate completely since there are still some Arab states, although a minority, which continue to maintain the secondary boycott. Others continue to maintain their ban on direct commercial exchanges with Israel. Nonetheless, I am convinced that sooner or later these last barriers will fall too.

"Against this background I would like to express to you my gratitude for your untiring efforts which helped facilitate achievement of this vital decision. In doing so, you served the interests of the Jewish community and the State of Israel and it gives me pleasure to write you this note to thank you for all your assistance."

The letter was signed "Shimon Peres, Minister of Foreign Affairs, State of Israel."

15

In France the boycott affair was over. Still, a mystery remained. Why had President Mitterrand decided to intervene in the L'Oréal affair? Why had he instructed his close advisers to put an end to the legal battle between Frydman and Dalle?

As with so much else in this case, the answer is found in the events of more than a half century ago. As the Frydman brothers pursued their research into France's murky past during World War II, they made a stunning discovery that went well beyond the L'Oréal affair and the boycott scandal.

When David Frydman first heard the name of Jacques Corrèze, he had started looking for information on La Cagoule. He diligently visited bookstores and libraries, asking questions and scrutinizing the existing books. He found very few mentions of the man. One Sunday, at the beginning of the summer of 1990, he decided to visit the *bouquinistes*, the picturesque stands along the Seine embankments where booksellers sell unusual books—rare editions, out-of-print volumes, and antique posters. With his wife, Lucienne, Frydman was walking on the Left Bank near the Place Saint-Michel when at one of the stands he discovered a thin brochure, written by a man named Joseph Désert, describing La Cagoule. He opened the booklet—and there was a full-page photograph of Jacques Corrèze.*

The bookseller, a young man with a short red beard, noticed Frydman's excitement and asked if he could help. When he heard what Frydman was looking for, he nodded. "Listen, you gotta go to the BDIC. They have great stuff there."

"What's the BDIC?"

"Bibliothèque de Documentation Internationale Contemporaine," the bookseller said.

This is the library of the Nanterre Faculty, one of the branches of the University of Paris, containing 1.5 million books, periodicals, and documents. David Frydman started working in the card index, and after several visits, in which he satisfied his curiosity about Corrèze, he decided to look up *La Terre Française*. This was a weekly magazine published in France during the German occupation. With a circulation of 83,000 copies, it was mostly marketed in the agrarian regions of France, but was on sale at newsstands in Paris and other big cities as well.

There was a compelling reason for his interest. David remembered that his brother Jean had mentioned *La Terre Française* after his luncheon with former president Gis-

---

* The French historian Jacques Delarue examined the booklet later and told Frydman that Joseph Désert did not exist. The brochure he had found was actually a police report on La Cagoule. Apparently some patriotic police officers, fearing that their explosive report might be buried because of political pressures, had chosen to publish it in the form of a booklet, signing it with a fictitious name.

card d'Estaing and his aide Sérisé in 1989. They had told Jean that an anarchistic magazine, *Le Crapouillot*, had recently reproduced a procollaborationist article published during the war in *La Terre Française*. The author of that article, printed in 1941, was a young man named André Bettencourt, the future owner of L'Oréal.

David had found *Le Crapouillot* and read the article. He couldn't believe his eyes. Dated October 11, 1941, Bettencourt's piece was titled "We Shall Denounce." Fiercely supportive of Marshal Pétain, it was an appeal to young people to expose the enemies of collaborationist Vichy.

> The Marshal has entrusted our youth with a large part of his hopes. . . . Shall we desert the Marshal at the crucial moment when one should be able to define oneself, even if one should make enemies? . . . The young people must be the agents of the Marshal in every village, I would gladly say the police of the Revolution. It is perhaps sad to visit this task of inquisition upon the youth. Somebody else should do it, but nobody else does. . . . When one must denounce for the common benefit, there should be no more camaraderie. . . . The denunciation . . . is a duty. This is a thankless task, but it is necessary. . . . For us, for France's recovery, we shall denounce the real culprits. Let's not ally ourselves with the devil!

In calling on French youth to become the regime's informers, this article brings to mind Nazism and Stalinism, both of which exhorted children to inform on their neighbors, friends, and parents.

David Frydman was sickened. André Bettencourt, the man widely known as Mitterrand's close companion in the dangerous years of the Resistance, had written this? How could André Bettencourt promote such a revolting idea? The owner of L'Oréal had been a minister in de Gaulle's and Mendès-France's cabinets. He was a member of the Académie des Beaux-Arts and a respected senator. He had been awarded the Resistance Medal. How could someone who preached to the youth to spy on people who opposed the pro-Nazi Pétain become a hero of the Resistance?

David Frydman's indignation was sincere, but what he discovered wasn't new. This article and another pro-Vichy piece had been reproduced years ago and even used against Bettencourt in one of his electoral campaigns. Still, nobody had tried to investigate Bettencourt's activities during the war.

David Frydman decided to find out if Bettencourt had published other articles in *La Terre Française*. The magazine wasn't included in the periodical card index, but Frydman found it in the "Public Life" category. He asked for all the issues and received two heavy volumes, one covering the years 1940–42 and the other 1943–44.

As he leafed through the old volumes, he soon discovered that André Bettencourt had been a regular contributor to the magazine. His weekly column was titled "*Ohé! Les Jeunes!*" (Hey, young men!) and even carried the drawing of a young, smiling Bettencourt. There were scores of his articles in the magazine, spread over twenty-one months.

With burning passion, week after week, Bettencourt attacked democracy, freedom, and real and imaginary enemies of the Vichy regime. With blind devotion he defended National Socialism.

"Our magazine doesn't mix in politics?" he asked rhetorically in July 1941. "You bet! This is untrue, absolutely untrue! We do mix in politics. We are proud of it and we shall always mix into the politics of France, France that is no longer embodied in a republic made of plaster, in a bust of Marianne,* but in a chief: PÉTAIN."

In several articles he poured his wrath on the Freemasons, considered by the pro-Nazi collaborators as enemies second only to Jews. In August 1941 a law against the Freemasons was promulgated, and Bettencourt immediately echoed pro-Nazi France's hatred, accusing the Masons of having "jeopardized our Christian civilization" and driven France "with growing speed toward a catastrophe." In the same article he raised a defense of Nazism:

> Let us not stupidly present Christianity and Nazism as opposed to each other. . . . The [German] revolutionary movement whose augury was National Socialist appears to us, much more than being a doctrine, as a world in motion, and an appeal for action. . . . This revolutionary current of the new Europe, coming from Germany, elevates us too. . . . May we benefit from the achievement of our neighbor, and as we couldn't be the cornerstone of this revolution, let us be at least its harmoniously sculpted keystone.

Bettencourt's admiration for Germany knew no limits. He spoke with adulation of the "historic meeting at Montoire" between Pétain and Hitler. He worshipped the German youth.

---

* Marianne, a female figure in Revolutionary garb, is the national symbol of the French Republic.

I remember having seen in Germany, a few months before the war, a youth camp dedicated to Ludwig van Beethoven . . . black and red buildings nestled on a hill's slope . . . a large gate of sculpted wood, and flying in the sky . . . an enormous flag with the Reich's colors. . . . Coming from the pine forest . . . I heard a song of extraordinary power and beauty. . . . The expression of an entire nation was coming at us in bursts.

That day, for the first time, I realized what a great people beside us . . . was doing for the body and soul of its youth. . . . That day I and the three friends with whom I traveled asked ourselves a few questions. Oh, we didn't ask each other aloud! No! But deep in our soul a secret chord vibrated; it was made of admiration, certainly, but also of bitterness and envy. What have they [the leaders of prewar France] done for our French youth, we thought. . . .

Why, here, is the youth the most beautiful attribute of the German nation, and why, in our country, is the youth kept out of sight?

In fact, André Bettencourt's trip, a tour of Belgium, Luxembourg, and Germany, had been made with four other friends: Pol Pilven, Bernard Duprez, François Dalle—and François Mitterrand. When they reached the youth camp, they were impressed by the disciplined young Germans. Their instructors had only to whistle and the docile youths marched, dived half-naked in a mountain lake, or sang romantic *Lieder*. The trip was described in the *Revue Montalembert*, but François Mitterrand's presence was not mentioned for a good reason: he had been drafted into the army a short while before and had left France without official authorization from his superiors. He later confirmed he had participated in the trip.

Bettencourt, emulating Nazi propagandists, vehemently accused the intellectuals and the academics for his country's troubles: "Let us condemn the treason of the professors and the writers and the demagogues, all these bad shepherds of our youth, all these 'civilization lovers.' "

And: "Absolute freedom leads to destruction. . . . Freedom is a slogan . . . a bluff, nonsense. . . . Freedom has never really existed."

In another pro-Nazi newspaper, *L'Élan*, Bettencourt issued a passionate call to erase "the three slogans of the Republic ['Liberty, Equality, Fraternity'] from our walls."

This was the real face of André Bettencourt that David Frydman discovered that day in Nanterre.

Frydman couldn't get authorization to photocopy the articles, for the librarians feared this might damage the dried paper. Therefore he diligently read and summarized most articles, and copied examples of Bettencourt's fiery prose. He showed the articles to Jean, who shared his amazement. They both understood the import of David's discovery, but many questions remained. What kind of magazine was *La Terre Française*? Did Bettencourt later acknowledge he had written for it, and did he ever express remorse for his pro-Nazi views? And how did Bettencourt get the Resistance Medal in spite of these articles? Jean and David Frydman decided to continue their research quietly.

One morning in the late fall of 1992, shortly after David completed his research in the Nanterre library, his car broke down and he decided to take the bus to his office. While waiting at the bus stop, he spotted a bookstore across the street. On an impulse he crossed the street and stopped before the shop window. In one corner he noticed a book he had never seen before: *L'Argent Nazi à la conquête de la presse française 1940–1944* (The Conquest of the French Press by Nazi Money, 1940–1944). He bought the book and found it to be a solidly researched, scholarly volume, written by a specialist in history and political science, Pierre-Marie Dioudonnat.

In it Frydman found several mentions of *La Terre Française*, and his disgust with Bettencourt increased when he discovered who had published the magazine. It had not been an independent publication or a Vichy propaganda organ. The magazine actually had been published by the German Propaganda Staffel, and had been directly financed by Goebbels's people in Berlin. A Nazi envoy, Dr. Hibbelen, had discreetly built a press empire in France, buying daily newspapers, weeklies, and monthlies, using French front companies and money from the coffers of the Reich. The main front was a small firm called Le Comptoir Financier Français. Later, the ties to Germany were no longer concealed, and representatives of the Propaganda Staffel, in and out of uniform, visited the headquarters of Hibbelen's press enterprises.

André Bettencourt had been on the payroll of the Propaganda ministry of Nazi Germany.

Frydman also learned that after France was liberated, the assets of the Comptoir Financier Français had been confiscated as enemy property and a threat to state security. The Propaganda Staffel had been declared by the Nuremberg Tribunal on War Crimes to be a criminal organization for its active participation in the Nazi crimes against humanity.

Frydman was very excited by his discovery. He

wouldn't even have known about the existence of the book if his car hadn't broken down that day and he hadn't happened to drift into "the one bookshop in the entire world," according to him, where the book was on display.

Soon thereafter he found in his office an invitation to a public symposium on museum management. It was being held on April 30, 1993, at the conference hall of the Fondation Singer Polignac at 21 avenue Georges-Mandel. The invitation stated that the debate would be chaired by André Bettencourt. Frydman decided to go.

The hall was very beautiful, decorated with paintings and flowers, and the meeting was attended by eighty well-dressed people. David Frydman didn't care what the meeting was about. He sat erect in his chair, not listening to the speakers, his eyes focused only on the gentleman who was moderating the debate. Tall, elegant, and very confident, he was always surrounded in the intermissions by admiring faces.

Frydman was deeply distressed. He was an emotional man, and the vicissitudes of the L'Oréal affair had badly affected his health, causing him a heart condition. The man he saw on the podium was the owner of L'Oréal, André Bettencourt, the supposed Resistance hero who had wanted France to become a country of Nazis.

When Bettencourt announced an open discussion, Frydman rose to his feet.

"My name is David Frydman, and I have two questions. In France there are a lot of Resistance museums, but I would like to build a Museum of the Collaboration. Who could advise me on that matter?"

One of the speakers casually gave him the name of a lady.

Frydman took a deep breath. "My second question is addressed to Monsieur Bettencourt. Mr. Bettencourt, you were active in collaboration. I have a set of your articles in *La Terre Française*. Would you agree to give me the manuscripts so I could place them in my museum?"

The question stunned and angered the audience. People furiously shouted at Frydman, waving their fists. He was booed by practically everybody. When the organizer of the symposium turned to Bettencourt and said, "Please don't answer," the audience reacted with an ovation.

Bettencourt, however, turned pale and left the room. He came back a short while later, fighting for composure. He said, "I am a public figure, I must answer." He went on, "It is true that I had the misfortune to write for *La Terre Française*, but I redeemed myself. I was in the Resistance. I even represented the National Council of Liberation in Geneva."

Frydman observed that Bettencourt was distraught and embarrassed. He had been compelled to admit his tainted past before his own friends. Still, he had behaved with dignity.

Frydman wasn't through with Bettencourt though. Shortly after the symposium, he asked his nephew Gilles Frydman to reexamine the volumes of *La Terre Française* in the Nanterre library and find out if there was any article of Bettencourt's David hadn't copied.

Gilles came back several hours later. "*La Terre Française* has disappeared," he said.

David Frydman filed a complaint with the library officials, but in vain. The magazine had vanished, as if somebody had wanted to erase it from France's memory. Frydman contacted several other libraries and documentation centers, in Paris and in the provinces, but the volumes of *La Terre Française* couldn't be found anywhere.

Determined to continue his pursuit, Frydman started touring various antiques fairs throughout France. At these fairs were always several stands that sold old books and magazines. In Chatou, Frydman was lucky again. He found a copy of *La Terre Française* from December 1940, printed on pink paper. Frydman was positive he hadn't seen this copy in Nanterre, for he would have remembered the color. The entire front page of the pink copy featured a single article, signed André Bettencourt.

David didn't like this new discovery. He now had to suspect that the volumes he had found at Nanterre had been expurgated already. Probably somebody had snipped quite a few pages from the collection he had seen. But where could he find another collection? He called the historian Jacques Delarue and told him about the disappearance of *La Terre Française* from Nanterre. Delarue replied that somebody might have intentionally moved the volumes to another rack. "They can stay there, undetected, for years." There was only one place where he still had a chance of finding the magazine, Delarue said—at the Bibliothèque Nationale.

At the National Library, Frydman was told he could not consult any of the magazine collections. The librarians explained to him that they were moving large portions of their archives from the rue Richelieu in Paris to Versailles. In a few weeks he might try there.

In the early summer of 1994 David Frydman drove to the historic city of Versailles, near Paris. Half wondering what new obstacle he would have to face, he walked into the reading room and asked for the magazine.

Yes, the librarian said, we have the full collection of *La Terre Française*.

David Frydman couldn't believe his ears. Nor his eyes when a library employee brought him the heavy, dusty volumes.

It was the full collection indeed, for there David Frydman saw an entire side to Bettencourt he hadn't found at Nanterre. There were two hateful onslaughts on the Jewish people.

David remembered that in the Bettencourt articles he had read at Nanterre, he hadn't noticed any mention of the Jews. For all the aversion he felt toward the pro-Nazi pieces, he'd had to admit that they didn't contain any anti-Semitic utterances. Frydman's thinking then had been that Bettencourt perhaps had been a fascist, but not an anti-Semite. Besides, his daughter had married a Jew.

But the new findings in Versailles cast another shadow on Mitterrand's companion in the Resistance. Bettencourt had saved his opinion of the Jews for the special color issues the magazine had printed on Easter and Christmas Eve.

"The Jews," he wrote for the Easter 1941 issue, "these hypocritical Pharisees, have no more hopes. For them, the story is ended. They have no faith. They don't carry in themselves the possibility of a recovery. Their race is tainted with Jesus's blood for all eternity. They will be damned by all. They have condemned God, without even wanting to recognize their ignominy, and to regret [what they have done]. . . . The Jews of today, not of race but of thought, are and will be vomited."

Bettencourt wrote in the Christmas issue: "The Jews believed they had won. They had succeeded in laying their hands on Jesus and crucifying him. Rubbing their hands, they shouted: 'Let his blood fall on us and on our children.' You know well how it fell on them and how it keeps falling. The instructions of the Eternal Book must be fulfilled."

The trail had not ended, however. Soon there would be explosive revelations that would shock all of France.

16

In 1994 the Frydman brothers got an advance copy of a book by a prominent French historian, Pierre Péan, called *Une Jeunesse française* (A French Youth). It related the hitherto unknown story of Mitterrand's right-wing connections during his youth and his activities as an official of the Pétain government in Vichy. A photograph, long concealed, appeared on the cover: Mitterrand and Pétain standing together, the young man admiringly looking at the old marshal.

The French people were appalled to learn that their Socialist president had been a collaborator of the Nazis. He had been a member of the Resistance less than a year! The French also discovered that Mitterrand had kept ties of close friendship with many former collaborators, including war criminals.

The book also contained the answers to the major questions that had preoccupied Jean and David Frydman for the last few years. It told, among other things, a tale of a chance friendship that had developed before the war. In the Paris of the early thirties, three young people met and became close friends. They still were in their teens, innocent, curious boys who had just arrived in the capital from the country. One of the youths was named François Dalle. The second was André Bettencourt. The third was none other than François Mitterrand.

Mitterrand was one of eight children of an affluent vinegar maker from the Charente *département* in the southwest of France, which is the home of cognac. In Paris, Mitterrand studied law and political science. Dalle, a brewer's son from the Pas-de-Calais on the Atlantic coast, was a law student as well. Bettencourt, a lawyer's son, had gone to the Saint-Joseph high school in the port of Le Havre.

The trio spent most of their time together, walking the picturesque streets of the Latin Quarter on the Left Bank, idling on the terraces of crowded Parisian cafés, mostly the fashionable Biarritz, courting their first loves, sharing their intimate secrets.

"We saw each other every day," Dalle said in an interview with Pierre Péan. "We walked together to law school every morning, and studied together at the law library." He and Mitterrand lived at a Catholic boarding house at 104 rue de Vaugirard. They studied together in the evening, had breakfast together in the morning, had lunch at a *pâtisserie* on the rue Saint-Jacques, and even spent their vacations together at each other's homes. For years Dalle recalled "the sweetness" of their summers at Mitterrand's home in Jarnac, and their pleasant boat trips. André Bettencourt was the last of the three to join their small group.

During his student years Mitterrand was attracted

to the right-wing political movements. Some rare photographs taken of the handsome youth during a right-wing student protest against foreigners, one tainted with racist and anti-Semitic sentiments, date from the time when the three friends were inseparable.

The close friendship of the three young men continued during the war.

Mitterrand was drafted into the French army, and a short while later he was taken prisoner by the Germans. After his release he joined Marshal Pétain's administration and was employed at the Vichy government department in charge of prisoners of war. In a peculiar essay entitled "Pilgrimage in Thuringia" that he published in a Pétainist and anti-Semitic review, *France, Revue de l'état nouveau*, in December 1942, Mitterrand blamed France's defeat on "the sinking regime, the unworthy [political] men, the [republican] institutions that were devoid of substance." An admirer of Marshal Pétain, he was even decorated with the Francisque, the highest order of the collaborationist regime.

Although he had Jewish friends, Mitterrand apparently wasn't bothered by their harrowing destiny in occupied France. Years later he claimed he hadn't known about the persecution of the Jews. That claim is difficult to believe. Every Vichy official was required to fill out several forms, one stating that he was not Jewish, another attesting that he did not belong to the order of Freemasons. For an alert young man who held a job in the Vichy administration, ignorance of the Jews' plight required being blind or deaf, and Mitterrand was neither. He had in fact turned down a job in the Department for Jewish Questions.

André Bettencourt was very close to Mitterrand during these years, while François Dalle was starting his career at Monsavon, one of the companies belonging to La Cagoule backer Eugène Schueller.

In a recent interview, Dalle described the beginning of his career. In July 1942, shortly after he got married, the young lawyer answered a newspaper ad in which Monsavon was seeking executives. *Et voilà tout.* There was no apparent association with Eugène Schueller. Dalle certainly was not a right-wing extremist. How then did he come under the wing of Eugène Schueller, the backer of La Cagoule and the man who preached war against the Jews? Perhaps the answer is, as others claim, that Dalle was hired by Schueller on the recommendation of André Bettencourt, who had become friendly with L'Oréal's boss and had praised him in a newspaper article.

While rising rapidly at Monsavon, Dalle joined the Resistance. Years later, he made contradictory assessments of his role in the underground. Sometimes he boasted he had been a Resistance member from the very start, "de première heure." On other occasions he spoke deprecatingly of his involvement. All he did, he said, was cross the boundary between occupied France and the free zone, carrying letters from families that had been separated from their relatives. He repeated those trips forty times. "This was risky business," he recalled years later, "but this was not Resistance."

It certainly wasn't Jean Frydman's kind of resistance.

After the war Dalle was appointed director general, then president, of L'Oréal. With his extraordinary talents he launched new products, restructured the cosmetics company, and opened subsidiaries abroad, transforming L'Oréal into a giant conglomerate. Besides selling L'Oréal's products directly to the public, it marketed them to thousands of beauty salons throughout the world. It gradually acquired competing companies and marketed their products under their original labels. During this early stage of its growth Schueller ran into trouble with the law because of his pro-Nazi activities during the war, but the charges were quietly dropped.

In 1950 Bettencourt married Schueller's daughter, Liliane, the heiress to Schueller's tremendous fortune. Overnight he became the richest man in France. He also became a rising star in French politics. He was elected to Parliament, then appointed a minister in the cabinet of the Jewish premier Pierre Mendès-France, and in several cabinets under the presidency of de Gaulle. He later became a senator and was elected to the prestigious Academy of Fine Arts.

The close friendship of Mitterrand, Dalle, and Bettencourt continued during the sixties and the seventies. When Mitterrand was elected to the presidency of France in 1981, he didn't forget his old friends. In 1986, he even suggested to Jacques Chirac that he appoint André Bettencourt as his minister of foreign affairs.

"Mitterrand," said Georges Kiejman, a former minister of his, "is a man of networks—networks of friendships and loyalty. He doesn't forsake his old friends, even those who have been banned by society."

This remark referred to the friendship Mitterrand maintained with René Bousquet. Mitterrand kept inviting him to the Élysée Palace even after Bousquet's despicable past became a matter of public knowledge.

In a side note, this strange sense of loyalty was extended as well to a central figure named in connection with the L'Oréal scandal: Jacques Corrèze.

The former "colonel" of the fascist Legion was a member of Mitterrand's extended family: the niece of Corrèze's wife, Edith Cahier, was the first wife of François Mitterrand's brother Robert. François Mitterrand had met Corrèze through Robert, and a close relationship developed between the two men.

When President Mitterrand visited the United States in 1984, he was the guest of honor at an intimate reception and dinner at the Hotel Pierre offered by the French community in New York. Jacques Corrèze, Cosmair's president, invited his deputy, Jean Lévy, to accompany him to the party. At the time Lévy, a Jew, had no idea of the Nazi past of his boss. The two stood in line, waiting to shake the president's hand. When Corrèze reached Mitterrand, the two men hugged each other closely.

Lévy would later recall their warm embrace with amazement. It was practically impossible that Mitterrand, one of the best informed men in France, could be unaware of Corrèze's ugly past.

The deep friendship between Mitterrand, Dalle, and Bettencourt provided the key to the question preoccupying the Frydman brothers: What had made the president of the French Republic intervene in the conflict between them and L'Oréal?

Bettencourt, interviewed at length in Péan's book, spoke of his activities in the Resistance at Mitterrand's side. He also described his friendship with Mitterrand before the war. Bettencourt's articles in *La Terre Française* and his past as a devout collaborator between 1940 and 1942 were not mentioned in Péan's book.

In a recent letter Bettencourt maintains that his "contacts" with the Resistance started at the end of 1942. According to an official history of the Mouvement National des Prisonniers de Guerre Déportés—National Movement of Deported Prisoners of War—Bettencourt had joined its clandestine activities against the Germans in November 1943. The MNPGD was led by François Mitterrand, who by this point had left Vichy and joined de Gaulle. Mitterrand had been in charge of the French

POWs when he was still a senior Vichy official, and he had good connections and a vast knowledge in this field. One of his ideas was to employ the POWs still imprisoned in camps in Germany as sources of intelligence and, perhaps, as a future auxiliary force to the Allies when they invaded the territory of the Reich.

After November 1943 Bettencourt often traveled with Mitterrand or on his behalf, and helped in liaison with other Resistance organizations. In December 1943, on one of these trips, Bettencourt was arrested in Nancy. He was released after a month thanks to the efforts of the local secretary of the MNPGD, Marie François. Shortly after Bettencourt's release, she was arrested and deported.

Whenever asked what exactly he did for the Resistance, Bettencourt spoke proudly of his assignment in Switzerland. He told Pierre Péan that in 1944 he was representing Mitterrand's MNPGD in Geneva as a member of the mission of the CNR, the Conseil National de la Résistance. Research has established that he indeed spent a little more than a month there, from mid-July to the third week of August, and in a letter to Eugène Schueller, Bettencourt spoke of "a month spent between Geneva and Bern."

Less clear is exactly why he went to Geneva. He told Péan he was in charge of liaison between that CNR mission and the one in Algiers, where de Gaulle's government was based at the time, "for all [matters] concerning the networks of [French] POWs in Germany, the parachute drops in France, the relations with the movement's emissaries in Algiers." To Schueller he wrote that he had done more or less what the MNPGD had asked him. "Two of my friends work for the same goals in Algiers. . . . It is a real satisfaction when one thinks of all that separated us materially."

Bettencourt also told Péan that he "maintained the liaison with the Americans and the British, especially with Allen Dulles of the OSS." He related how in Geneva he met Allen Dulles, the European station chief of the American Office of Strategic Services,* which was based in Switzerland. Dulles took Bettencourt to his office and showed him several safes full of money, earmarked to finance the European resistance movements. In the meantime the Allied forces, which had landed in Normandy on June 6, 1944, were advancing toward Paris. On August 15 another Allied task force landed in the south of France. Dulles decided to come to France, and according to Bettencourt he took him along for the ride in his car. In a letter written many years later to American congressman Eliot L. Engel, Bettencourt specified that Allen Dulles was on his way to join the Allied armies after their landing in the south.

In August 1944, Bettencourt told Péan, he also participated in the liberation of Paris with his friends François Dalle and François Mitterrand. Their headquarters there were in the offices of the Commissariat Général aux Prisonniers de Guerre on rue Meyerbeer.

Bettencourt's record seems very impressive. Yet in his official *curriculum vitae* published in *Who's Who*, the years 1940–46 were left blank. In 1946, the book states, Bettencourt was elected a local councilman in Lillebonne, near Le Havre.

How had Bettencourt met Eugène Schueller? Bettencourt maintains that he met the tycoon in 1938 on the recommendation of "a journalist friend." That same day he met Schueller's daughter, Liliane. If the story is true,

---

* Later he was to become the chief of the U.S. Central Intelligence Agency. His brother, John Foster Dulles, was President Eisenhower's secretary of state.

it is probable that Bettencourt introduced his friend François Dalle to Schueller a few years later. David Frydman's research discovered a trace of the Bettencourt-Schueller relationship in *La Terre Française*. The young columnist was deeply impressed by Schueller and sang his praises in a special editorial published in his magazine on December 6, 1941.

"I gave [a young man] the remarkable book of a friend of mine, Monsieur E. Schueller, entitled *The Revolution of the Economy*. This [is a] book that all the industrialists of tomorrow and today should read. This is a young person's book par excellence."

Actually, in this book Schueller exposed his corporatist-fascist economic ideas, well suited to the "new order" in Europe. His book disdained French democratic institutions and leaders in favor of the structures and economy of Nazi Germany. Schueller wrote: "The [workers'] unions have no right to exist in a communal and authoritarian state that functions well.

"The only courageous solution of a strong government is doing what the Germans did: abolish the unions and incorporate all the workers in a work front."

The book, printed by Denoël, was presented as second on the list of the series World Revolution. The first was *Speeches* by Adolf Hitler.

However, after 1942, the year when he had broken with La Cagoule's founder Eugène Deloncle, Schueller kept a low profile. During 1943, as the tide began to turn toward the Allies, it became clear to more and more people that Germany was going to be defeated. Like so many of his countrymen, Schueller discreetly crossed the line and became a supporter of the anti-Nazi struggle. When his friend Bettencourt surreptitiously arrived in Geneva, using the war name of Grainville, he carried a letter from Schueller to L'Oréal's subsidiary in Switzerland. Schueller had offered to finance, through L'Oréal, Bettencourt's stay in Geneva, but Bettencourt ultimately didn't need that money, instead using funds given to him by the Resistance.

Still, why had Bettencourt gone to Geneva? David and Jean Frydman spoke to the historian Jacques Delarue and to the Resistance hero Colonel Ravanel. They then interviewed two former officials of the Conseil National de la Resistance—Robert Chambeiron, a CNR archivist, and Daniel Cordier, secretary to the late CNR founder, Jean Moulin. Both stated formally that their organization had never had a mission in Geneva. Bettencourt, therefore, couldn't have been a member of such a mission. In fact, he later would admit that he must have made a mistake about the name of the mission.

Further, his claim that he was a friend of Allen Dulles seems peculiar, for in Dulles's personal papers in the Mudd Library at Princeton University, neither Bettencourt nor Grainville is ever mentioned.

One Frenchman who frequently corresponded with Dulles after the war was General Pierre de Benouville, a Resistance hero who had been in close contact with Dulles during the war. But here too no mention was made of Bettencourt. When Allen Dulles died in March 1969, a funeral service in his memory was held at the American Cathedral in Paris. General de Benouville sent a detailed letter about the service to Allen Dulles's widow, with a list of her husband's friends and acquaintances who had attended. Bettencourt was not among the twenty former resistants and freedom fighters who came, nor among those who sent their condolences to the widow.

The story that Bettencourt came back to France in Allen Dulles's car also seems questionable. According to

his biography by Peter Grose, Allen Dulles crossed the
Swiss border into France on August 29 and headed for
Lyon, where he planned to catch a plane for London. He
never intended to join the Allied forces that had landed in
the south. In Lyon he was surprised to meet the OSS director, Major General William "Wild Bill" Donovan, who
had landed at St.-Tropez and headed north, hoping to establish contact with Dulles. They spent a few days at a *Maquis*
safe house before commandeering an aircraft to London.

This surreptitious trip across unsafe French territory
was the only one Dulles made. The OSS spymaster, Peter
Grose writes, "was moving with one of his resistance
agents toward the airport at Lyons." For the purpose of
this journey, Dulles probably needed a field agent, a man
who knew the region well and had good contacts with the
local population. It seems almost certain that Bettencourt
was not this agent.

Finally, Bettencourt was not present at the liberation
of Paris. In a letter to Schueller of September 27, 1944,
he wrote, "It is for me a sadness to have been absent from
Paris during the great coup that I had helped prepare before my departure with Patrice [Roger Pelat] who has become a colonel in the meantime."

So what did Bettencourt do in Geneva? The truth was
exposed by *Le Monde*'s executive editor, Edwy Plenel, in
the form of two letters from Bettencourt to his friend François Mitterrand. The letters were published on March 9,
1995.

Bettencourt, alias Grainville, wrote to Mitterrand, alias
Morland, on August 9, 1944:

My dear François,
    When I departed, you directed me, among other
things, to establish contact as soon as possible with

the English and American representatives in Geneva in order to interest them in what we already had done in Germany and to find out in what way they would agree to help us. When I arrived in Geneva, I immediately informed the delegation of my wish to establish contact with them.

Since, three weeks have passed during which three telegrams . . . have arrived to remind me, if needed, of the orders you had given me. I asked myself by what method I could take any action. A first meeting with the American representative had been fixed for me by Martel, but for reasons independent of me it didn't take place. All of a sudden, last Monday, I got a phone call from General D., inviting me to join him in order to visit Mr. Perrichon [the war name of Max Schoop, an aide of Allen Dulles], who wanted to see me urgently.

This first conversation and the two others that followed were extremely sympathetic and cordial. To be precise, the situation concerning the interior German front can be summarized in this manner: Mr. Perrichon, the American representative here, puts at the disposal of our movement 2,500,000 francs. You'll receive by the bearer of this letter 350,000 francs in cash. By the intermediary of a bank, L.V. will put at your disposal, from him to you, rapidly I hope, the sum of 1,500,000 francs in French money. This compensation is already in transaction. The rest of the money will be sent to you directly in marks valid in Germany, to avoid redundant transactions in Paris.

This sum of 2,500,000 francs is addressed to you by the Americans as a first token of trust and sympathy in order to help us with the departures that might

take place during this month, until you give your
agreement in principle to present a more complete
budget for the coming months. I suggest that you con-
vey right away to Mr. Perrichon and through him to
his government our thanks to all of them for this first
aid in this action that you already have undertaken in
spite of the enormous difficulties and lack of means.

The terms of the agreement with the Americans, Bettencourt explained, were that "it is understood with Mr.
Perrichon . . . that representatives of the movement will
go to Germany as soon as possible in order to insti-
gate there a direct participation in the Resistance and an
intelligence-gathering organization to the limits of
possibility." The operations conceived by the Americans,
he wrote, were to use the "ten million foreigners" held
by force in German territory; "a military action on
D-Day"; "carrying out acts of sabotage now by the workers in industrial installations"; and "organize an intelligence circuit through prisoners in kommandos and the
STG men."

What he still had to do, Bettencourt concluded, was
establish contact with the British representative in Switzerland to find out in what way the British authorities
could also help. He intended to ask "Mr. Perrichon" to
put him in touch with his British colleague.

Two days later, Bettencourt sent another letter to Mitterrand, informing him of an impending meeting with the
British. "It will happen sooner or later because I want it,
and I assure you that everything I undertake to do with
the Allies will be carried out absolutely to the letter, which
will allow me to ask them in return if not for the greatest
trust, at least for full respect. We must do everything in
complete accord with our allies so that, from this com-

munity of purpose, we all emerge stronger and united by the liberation of France and the victory of all."

These letters were matched by a secret dispatch, IN-16846, sent on August 9 by Allen Dulles in Bern to William Donovan, the chief of the Office of Strategic Services. From this dispatch, kept in the National Archives in Washington, it is clear that Allen Dulles did not meet Bettencourt or show him safes full of money. The ciphered telegram reads:

284 [code for Max Schoop, Dulles's aide] reports as follows concerning his discussions with Grainville, who represents . . . MNPGD. This man was in Geneva not long ago. Beginning last winter, we have been trying to influence MNPGD along the following lines: A. Preparation for direct action by workers and prisoners as soon as the time is ripe. B. Establishment of a system of secret intelligence through the workers.

Although their funds are insufficient, MNPGD has already made contact with groups in 45 out of 60 Nazi prisoner camp areas and also has around 30 inspectors going in and out of France. Among these are some individuals who travel under official Vichy protection. Approximately 15 assistants are assigned to each regional leader, and these agents operate under cover of proved liaison men between the Nazi control staffs and the prisoners. Not long ago, MNPGD dispatched representatives under this same cover to circulate among the French workers in the Reich.

It is thought that this organization is sufficiently well organized to stimulate current sabotage and to unite the eventual French resistance in the Reich. They are ready to increase their activities to bring about these measures if they receive monetary backing equal in round numbers to 10,000,000 French francs each month. These funds are to be used for travelling expenses, reserve funds for men in camps and for bribery.

The scheme would include dropping food, arms, and other supplies by parachute at previously designated camps on D-Day. In addition, it is hoped that arrangements can be made for this group to continue to operate in the Reich even if France is made inaccessible by the battle lines. . . .

We feel that this movement may be developed more practically through France than directly from Bern. Following is from 110 [Allen Dulles]: Because the matter is imperative and since there is not time to wait for an answer from you because of the early departure of the courier, I propose to advance a sum equal to 2–3 million French francs, a portion of which will be in Nazi currency, to expedite the work mentioned in the above paragraphs. I should be grateful for your orders concerning additional financing and also your views on the material discussed in this cable.

This cable from Allen Dulles divulged the true objectives of Bettencourt's mission to Geneva. He came to get money from the American and British secret services. He acted under pressing orders of François Mitterrand, whose aides kept sending him telegrams repeating his instructions. Bettencourt tried to obtain 10,000,000 French francs a month for the rest of the war.

He apparently made a good impression on Max Schoop, whom he met on August 9. He received the first payment of 2.5 million francs, which he immediately transferred to Mitterrand. But what happened to the money? For what ends was it used? Neither Bettencourt nor Mitterrand ever supplied an answer to that question. We know only that there was no revolt of French prisoners in Germany. We also know that when Bettencourt returned to Paris, the city had already been liberated. Mitterrand had been appointed secretary general of the department of prisoners of war in the first free cabinet. Bettencourt got a job on the minister's staff.

The contacts with the OSS did not continue, and nothing came of them. In the end, Bettencourt's Switzerland trip had only two tangible results: The first is that 2.5 million francs were moved from the OSS coffers into some unknown war chest in Paris. The second is that Bettencourt was officially recognized as a Resistance member and was awarded a medal for his valiant exploits by François Mitterrand.

The complex story of three friends, bound by shadowy ties, does not end here, though. More quid pro quo was forthcoming.

By the early winter of 1944, Mitterrand, now married, had resigned from his position as secretary general of the POW department, and had no income. He spoke about it with his longtime friends, François Dalle and André Bettencourt. Dalle was now director general of the Monsavon factory owned by Eugène Schueller, and Bettencourt too had become very close to Schueller.

Dalle and Bettencourt spoke to Schueller, who had met Mitterrand several times. Mitterrand apparently wasn't bothered by the fact that at this time Schueller was the subject of two separate investigations for his collaborationist activities during the war.

Schueller agreed to help, and the twenty-seven-year-old François Mitterrand was appointed editor in chief of the women's magazine *Votre Beauté* published by the L'Oréal group. This was the only job outside politics Mitterrand ever took. He also became a member of the board of the Société d'Editions Modernes Parisiennes and the Editions du Rond Point, Schueller's companies that published *Votre Beauté* and other magazines.

This is not to say Mitterrand was happy with his new job. He didn't care very much for cold creams and nail polish. Still, he now enjoyed a comfortable income. For a while he planned to become a publisher and establish a prestigious publishing house. He toyed with the idea of transforming *Votre Beauté* into a literary review. The directors of the magazine, however, were determined to keep it a periodical focused mainly on cosmetics.

By the summer of 1945 Mitterrand's relations with the directors of the magazine had become strained. His friendship with Bettencourt and Dalle hadn't suffered, though. That same year Bettencourt made him a cofounder of a new agricultural newspaper, *La France agricole*.

No articles in *Votre Beauté* were ever signed by Mitterrand, but his thumbprints could be easily detected in some editorials, and Pierre Péan discovered that he wrote for the magazine under the pseudonym Frédérique Marnais. One of the Marnais articles was particularly poignant, as it tenderly spoke of the wonderful experience of raising a baby. That was soon after Mitterrand's firstborn son had died at the age of three months.

Finally, Mitterrand left *Votre Beauté* and ran for a parliamentary seat. In his campaign in the Nièvre district he was apparently helped, both financially and politically, by Eugène Schueller. Mitterrand willingly accepted this assistance, and the ensuing victory started him on the long political road leading to the presidential palace.

After Mitterrand became president of France, members of the parliamentary opposition used this chapter from his past to attack him on the floor of the National Assembly. One of them, Alain Madelin, sparked the wrath of Mitterrand's Socialist supporters on February 2, 1984, by proposing to explore the question: "What did François Mitterrand do after the war?" He answered that the Socialist leader had become "an editor, directing a magazine called *Votre Beauté*." He added, to cheers from the right-wing opposition: "I'll invite the historians to check who was the owner [of this magazine] at the time." He meant, of course, La Cagoule sponsor Eugène Schueller.

Another member of Parliament, Pierre de Benouville, rushed to the podium to succor Mitterrand. Benouville was one of the great French heroes of the war. His titles were impressive: brigadier general, Companion of the Liberation, Knight of the Legion of Honor, member of the 'executive committee of the underground National Liberation Movement, chief of external relations for the Resistance. Although belonging to a right-wing party, the Gaullist RPR, Benouville had been a close friend of Mitterrand's since early childhood and remained a devoted follower. In a highly emotional speech Benouville praised Mitterrand's record and reminded the Assemblée Nationale of the president's glorious past in the Resistance.

This speech in Parliament was not the first time Pierre de Benouville had come to the aid of Mitterrand in connection with Schueller. He had already done that in the late forties, when Eugène Schueller had found himself in desperate need of Mitterrand's help.

Shortly after Paris was liberated in August 1944, grave charges were lodged against Eugène Schueller for collaboration with the enemy. The charges were brought before two different institutions, acting separately.*

One was the recently created Comité Régional Interprofessionnel d'Epuration dans les Entreprises—Regional Interprofessional Committee for the Purge of Industry. Their duty was to investigate the activities of former collaborators in different companies. They submitted their conclusions to the regional prefect, who in turn submitted them to the local court of justice, which could initiate a criminal proceeding.

The second institution investigating Schueller was the Paris police.

The purge committee carried out most of its work in 1946. The charges brought against Schueller were:

1. Having organized in his factories tendentious [procollaborationist] lectures
2. Having financially backed [Deloncle's] MSR
3. Having published under the German occupation a book, *The Revolution of the Economy*, favorable to the application of the Work Charter,† and hostile to the unions
4. Having economically collaborated with the Germans
5. Having facilitated the departure of workers to Germany
6. Having maintained relations with notorious collaborators

* While researching another subject, the author gained access to the files of the Schueller investigations, which had been closed since the late forties.

† The Work Charter was a document issued by the Vichy government that set forth the regime's political and economic principles, which emulated fascist corporate theories.

Schueller countered these charges by claiming that he had been an active member of the Resistance since the beginning of the German occupation, and had financially helped Resistance networks and dissidents, protected people who refused to work in Germany, and helped Jews and prisoners to escape.

The charges were first discussed by the professional section of the chemical industries, a part of the larger Comité d'Epuration. It heard various witnesses on June 13 and July 4. Testimony in favor of Schueller was brought before the section by General Pierre de Benouville, who asked to testify on his own initiative.

In 1943, I wanted to establish contact with several industrialists. I was on a mission for the [French provisional] government in Algeria. The first industrialist I met was Mr. Schueller. He had been introduced to me by [future member of Parliament] Max Brusset. . . . Schueller had agreed to help me by all means.

I didn't see Mr. Schueller again because the meeting place became known to the Gestapo, which arrested my assistants. That prevented Schueller from coming. . . .

I heard that Mr. Schueller had to appear before you, and I want to assist him with my testimony.

I know his affection for the "proportional salary."* He spoke about it on the radio. This is his baby. He spoke about it to Pétain, Laval, Blum, and others.

Mr. Schueller promised to give us [the Resistance] two million.

---

* The proportional salary was a new structure for workers' wages, based on a base salary and a proportional share of the company's profits, that had been conceived by Schueller in the thirties.

Benouville's testimony was rather thin. All he could say about Schueller was that he had met him once, and had been promised money.

Still, the section concluded that Schueller had not been a collaborator. It suggested that the owner of L'Oréal be cleared.

When the case moved up the ladder, though, and came before the Comité d'Epuration itself, the charges against Schueller were regarded seriously. On November 6, 1946, the committee found Schueller guilty of all charges and stated that his acts of resistance didn't extenuate his guilt. The committee agreed that Schueller deserved the harshest sentence that it was authorized to pass, and recommended that Schueller "be forbidden to hold a position of management in industry; forbidden to be a member of the board or of a supervision board in a commercial company; forbidden to exercise the powers of management or administration in an associate position, for having helped enemy goals by his public stand during the occupation."

The committee also recommended that the case be transferred to the court of justice in order to bring Schueller to trial.

The recommendations were conveyed to the prefect, who immediately prepared a decree confirming the verdict of the committee.

But then General Pierre de Benouville intervened again.

On November 14, 1946, eight days after the Comité d'Epuration reached its verdict, Benouville walked into the office of the general secretary of the purge committees, a Mr. Jouannet. He vigorously defended Eugène Schueller, citing his activities in the Resistance and his help to many underground organizations. He claimed to have benefited personally from Schueller's services and

stressed that he had deeply appreciated this help. Benouville claimed that only Schueller's theory of the "proportional salary" had brought upon him all his troubles, but
"his anti-German action was a very serious counterbal-
ance to some possibly imprudent utterances."

Benouville then asked to meet the prefect in order to
"present some important points" concerning Schueller.

The secretary general was deeply impressed. General
de Benouville was a legendary hero, a personal adviser to
the army minister. In spite of his pressing duties he had
found the time to intervene for Eugene Schueller. Jouannet dispatched a detailed report to the prefect of the Seine
district.

Five days later, Benouville telephoned again to inform
the secretary general he was leaving for Germany for a
few days but was returning the following week, and he
wanted to see the prefect. He reminded the secretary general that several well-known former members of the Resistance had testified in favor of Schueller. He also sent
the prefect, by special messenger, a copy of Schueller's
book *The Revolution of the Economy*, and claimed that
other economists had published similar theories and had
not been bothered.

The prefect met Benouville on his return and yielded
to his pressure. In an unprecedented move he sent Eugène
Schueller's file back to the Comité d'Epuration and asked
them to review the case. He openly admitted that he was
doing so because of General de Benouville's intervention.

The purge committee met on June 24–25, 1947, and
decided to acquit Schueller of all charges. It based the
decision on "new elements of appreciation that had not
been known to the committee during its deliberations of
November 6, 1946." Nothing was said as to the nature
of these new elements.

The committee concluded: "In light of the new facts and information, especially the participation of the accused in acts of resistance against the occupier, it is found that Schueller didn't act, during the occupation, with the conscious intention of helping enemy goals."

Further down in the committee's conclusion was an analysis of the charges against Schueller. His financing of the MSR was not mentioned. Deloncle, Corrèze, Filliol, La Cagoule, the RNP did not appear. Omitted were his articles in the collaborationist revue *L'Atelier*. Also missing was the fact that he had gone to the Reich embassy in Paris to declare his allegiance to Hitler as "the Führer of Europe."

In a mockery of justice the committee pronounced that "from the first to the last day of the occupation, Schueller proved he was a good patriot and took an active part in the Resistance."

There is no doubt that Benouville had been asked to intervene in favor of L'Oréal's founder. Why else would this French hero go out of his way to help someone he had met only once in his life? There seems to be only one person whose influence over Benouville was such that he would agree to plead for Eugène Schueller—François Mitterrand.

Mitterrand, who was deeply indebted to Schueller and whose friends Dalle and Bettencourt were intimately involved with the magnate, was no longer the jobless young man who, three years before, had to accept a position he hated at *Votre Beauté*. He had become a force to reckon with, elected to Parliament—with Schueller's help—on November 10, 1946. Two months later, Prime Minister Paul Ramadier would name Mitterrand his minister for veterans affairs.

———

The second investigation of Eugène Schueller led to an even more appalling cover-up.

On August 29, 1944, a few days after the liberation of Paris, a group of L'Oréal workers filed a complaint against Schueller at a police station. This complaint, which was anonymous, was soon followed by several others, signed by workers and executives at L'Oréal. Schueller was accused of collaborating with the Germans, of financing Deloncle and the MSR, of exhorting, on the radio, young Frenchmen to go to work in Germany, and of making tainted profits by selling the products of his plants to the Germans.

On November 30, 1945, an investigation report was submitted by Inspector Louis Bornand of the Sûreté Nationale, a branch of the interior ministry roughly comparable to the FBI. The report was damning, describing Schueller's important role in La Cagoule and his alliance with Deloncle, as well as most of Schueller's collaborationist activities. Still, Inspector Bornand noted, at the liberation Schueller had been questioned by the Free French, but was released after proving that he had financed an underground Resistance group in the Puy-de-Dôme.

Other reports also established Schueller's guilt. The Sûreté Nationale informed the Paris police in February 1947 that Schueller was simultaneously under investigation in connection with the trial of Marshal Pétain; the inquiry into the MSR; and the activities of Inter-France, the press agency financed by the Germans during the war.

The police interrogated scores of witnesses for the prosecution and the defense. But as time passed, the accusations faded away and new documents appeared in Schueller's voluminous file. What tipped the balance, apparently, were a few letters.

The first was written by the indefatigable Benouville,

dated December 27, 1946. "I used information supplied by Monsieur Schueller from 1942 to March 1944," the general wrote, "by the intermediary of Max Brusset, alias Montherlant, today member of Parliament from the Charente-Maritime.

"Mr. Schueller's main task was, on one hand, to obtain certain secret and confidential documents like those emanating from the pro-German agency Inter-France and on the other hand to supply us with information about the industrial milieux." Benouville then related again the famous meeting with Schueller that hadn't taken place. At that meeting Schueller was supposed to deliver a report to him, which he did not.

This letter might have stood up to scrutiny if not for a letter to the police from Max Brusset himself. Brusset, the man who had introduced Schueller to Benouville during the war, stated that this took place at the beginning of 1943. The general thus could not have used Schueller in 1942; he didn't know him yet. Brusset added that "many contacts were maintained with Monsieur Schueller through a channel with Monsieur de Benouville." But Benouville had stated in his letter that Brusset had been the intermediary. So who had maintained the contacts? Were there any contacts?

Brusset did note Schueller's help for his information services, claiming that through Schueller's companies, "we subscribed to Inter-Radio, and various official and informal publications, which allowed us to obtain an abundant information on the German propaganda." But Inter-Radio and Inter-France were official sources of information. There was nothing "secret and confidential" about them—anyone could get their communiqués.

Brusset also testified about Schueller's willingness to

finance Resistance activities. This suggests rank opportunism. Starting in 1943, Schueller had begun weaving a safety net by giving money to various Resistance emissaries. One of the witnesses against him even claimed that he used L'Oréal for collaborating with the Germans, while the chiefs of his other factory, Monsavon, were busy cooperating with the Resistance.

Following the letters of Benouville and Brusset, a detailed report was filed by Michel Robinet, an accountant, for the *juge d'instruction* in charge of the Schueller case. Robinet did not limit his report to checking Schueller's accounts but also reviewed his political activities. On pages 26–28 of his report, he stated that Schueller's name was mentioned neither in the documents of the MSR nor in the list of its members. Robinet concluded that he either had not been a member or had left the MSR very early.

Robinet also cleared Schueller both of financing La Cagoule and of trading with the Germans. He conceded that Schueller had first approved of sending his workers to Germany, but when he learned the ugly truth about that operation he had refused to support it anymore.

The last element in Schueller's file was a pair of letters from André Bettencourt. The first had been sent on January 29, 1944, shortly after Bettencourt, now working for Mitterrand, had been released from Nancy prison.

"A friend of mine who is going to Paris," Bettencourt wrote, "will deliver to you this short letter upon his arrival. You'll find my very deep gratitude for your hospitality three days ago. You were one of those to whom I wanted to give a sign of life as early as possible."

Bettencourt described his sojourn in prison, the heroism of his comrades, "and especially the one that arranged my release." He spoke highly of the other prisoners he met and stressed how fortunate he was to be free again. He wrote that his experience in jail was "tough, but excellent."

> I hope, though, that you have been spared such an experience. You shared with me your fears. Various conversations [I had] before my departure from Paris make me believe they unfortunately are quite justified. Be therefore very careful. You are terribly impulsive in everything, but I believe that the support you have given to many of us must be protected, and these friendships must not be known, absolutely. If you were compromised, those who approach you might find themselves in a more delicate situation. . . .
>
> Your help has been personally useful to me more than once. Thank you very much again, but frankly, I think you ought to overcome all these difficulties, this is the country's interest. It is better to prepare, for better times, the [economic] program which is so dear to you, and which perhaps you shouldn't discuss so early.

The letter was signed "De Bettencourt."

This letter is of doubtful validity. Submitted to an expert on the period, it was qualified by him as a *lettre de complaisance*—meaning it had been written much later in order to furnish Schueller with an alibi.

"One didn't write letters like that and sign them with his real name during the war," the expert said. "Bettencourt could as well have added a request to German Gestapo agents not to open the letter if it fell into their hands! As for the substance, it is a clumsy attempt to prove that Schueller used to express anti-German views at this period."

The second letter from André Bettencourt was dated September 27, 1944. Bettencourt thanked Schueller for offering him financial help during his mission to Switzerland. The letter had been sent from Paris, on Bettencourt's return. He wrote with enthusiasm of his return to the liberated Paris.

> I found here Mitterrand and all my friends. . . . I hope now that we'll be able to meet again those of ours who are "there" [in Germany]. It would be such a party!
>
> I was pleased to learn from François that finally you didn't have any difficulties. It is very disconcerting, for me, to be able to walk the streets without taking precautions. It seems to me we're getting away with it. . . .

There are doubts raised by this second letter as well, although it seems authentic. It was apparently adduced by Schueller to prove he had helped the Resistance in Geneva.

The testimonies piled up. On December 6, 1948, the government commissioner for prosecution wrote a brief on Schueller's case. The commissioner formally established that L'Oréal and Monsavon had made no profits from selling their products to Germany during the war. He then examined the accusations of political collaboration. He stated that Schueller had indeed collaborated in 1940–41, but he accepted all of Schueller's explanations. The commissioner described Schueller's "personal activities for the liberation of our country."

Schueller had aided the Resistance, the commissioner wrote, rescued Jews and dissidents, contributed important sums to underground movements, and "even agreed to run certain personal risks by serving as an agent of liaison and intelligence for General de Benouville of the Libération Nationale movement."

The commissioner decided to drop all charges.

17

Tenacious and dedicated, the Frydman brothers pursued their personal war against L'Oréal. They had already spent a fortune on research and lawyers' fees, and they had lost considerable income in France and abroad, since revenue from their film libraries had been hurt by the Paravision affair. They kept fighting, writing letters, courting the media, suing and being sued.

Their attacks were not indiscriminate, though. In America, angry Jewish women had smashed crateloads of perfume and creams and lotions, bottle by bottle, in front of Cosmair's headquarters; many had called for a boycott on L'Oréal products. The Frydman brothers demurred, saying they weren't at war with the entire company. They were fighting what Jean Frydman had named "the parallel L'Oréal," the shadowy organization that had given refuge to Corrèze and a string of former collaborators.

Corrèze was dead, François Dalle was gone. But the man at the top still remained. The richest man in France, the former collaborator. They wanted to force André Bettencourt out of L'Oréal and out of his political citadel, the Senate. He was their last but most formidable rival.

On October 11, 1994, the Frydman brothers printed and circulated a slim red volume titled *Pour servir la mémoire*—To Serve Memory. Its subtitle was: André Bettencourt and the Pro-Nazi Tradition.

The foreward summarized in a few paragraphs the Frydman brothers' struggle against L'Oréal and the boycott.

> But this combat . . . became much more serious as things progressed. A new dimension emerged, even more unbearable: the presence of Nazi criminals in the managing structure of L'Oréal. . . .
>
> We were conscious of our weakness in facing a multinational company, the number-one advertiser, belonging to the richest family in France and surrounded by a flurry of lawyers and "advisers." Not to mention its relations with everyone "in high places."
>
> We found out that André Bettencourt had been a collaborator. We found several articles with a very troubling content. But almost all the documents concerning his past during that period had vanished. This was not by chance. A few days ago we finally found his articles and the Nazi magazine in which they were published. Today, we can state and prove that Monsieur Bettencourt was, for twenty-one months, an active agent of the Propaganda Staffel, and that he published articles that supported National Socialism, and called for the annihilation of the Jews, the Freemasons, and the resistants, all of them defined as criminals. . . .
>
> We present all this without seeking revenge, but with the purpose of having contributed to the Preservation of Memory.

The brochure described the relations between Bettencourt and the Propaganda Staffel and quoted anti-Semitic and pro-Nazi passages from Bettencourt's articles. Many of his pieces were reproduced in the brochure. After a considerable effort David Frydman had obtained the Versailles librarians' authorization to take photographs of *La Terre Française*. He had driven there several times a week, accompanied by relatives and equipped with a stand, cameras, and lights. They had spent the summer photographing every single article signed by André Bettencourt.

The red book also described the relations between Bettencourt and Schueller. It contained a succinct account of Eugène Schueller's political past, marked by the cabals of La Cagoule and the violence of Deloncle, Filliol, and Corrèze. The narrative was supported by abundant documentation. In its last part the red book dealt with the notorious Nazis who had found a safe haven at L'Oréal after the war, people like Jean Azéma, Henri Deloncle, Jean Filliol, Jacques Piquet, and Jacques Corrèze.

The Frydman brothers printed the red book in Israel and shipped it to France so that it couldn't be seized by a court order. They then sent it to a select mailing list of Jewish organizations in France and the United States, as well as to intellectuals, writers, and political figures.

On November 30, 1994, a few days after receiving the red book, U.S. Congressman Eliot L. Engel wrote a letter.

Dear Mr. Bettencourt:

As you know, any request for a visa into the territory of the United States . . . requests a truthful response to the following question:

". . . Between 1933 and 1945 were you involved

in any way in persecutions associated with Nazi Germany or its allies?"

As a member of the U.S. House of Representatives' Foreign Affairs Committee, information has come to my attention which suggests that the negative responses you have made to this inquiry in connection with the numerous times you have entered the United States may not have been accurate.

Engel then described Bettencourt's articles in *La Terre Française* and quoted the violently anti-Semitic paragraphs. He singled out Bettencourt's article of Christmas 1941, in which he had written, "The Jews . . . succeeded in laying their hands on Jesus to crucify him. Rubbing their hands, they shouted: 'Let his blood fall on us and on our children.' You know well how it fell on them and how it keeps falling. The instructions of the Eternal Book must be fulfilled."

Engel wrote:

The plain meaning of this shocking statement is a call for genocide against the Jews. As a result of the atrocities of the Nazis and their French collaborators, 75,000 French Jews and thousands of other targets of Nazi hatred, such as the Freemasons, against whom several of your columns also were directed, perished.

I request that you send me full particulars, as to your association with the *Propaganda Staffel* and its publications, your ties to fascist or Nazi organizations during the period 1939–45, a full set of your public writings during the war years and any other material you believe relevant so that I may assess what steps should be taken respecting your continued access to the United States.

Almost two months later, on January 25, 1995, Bettencourt replied in a long and detailed letter.

> I do not remember the question on applications for a United States visa asking whether the applicant has been involved in Nazi persecutions, in part because I generally used a diplomatic passport . . . and in part because a member of my government staff would have attended to visa matters for me. If I ever completed such a visa application, I surely answered that question in the negative and believe that I would have been correct in doing so. . . .
>
> I do not deny . . . having written articles for *La Terre Française* in 1941–42, and I have never ceased regretting having done so. The articles, however, were never intended as a call to genocide and are not able to be interpreted as such.

Bettencourt said he was twenty-two years old and living in Normandy when he wrote for *La Terre Française.* He sent his articles to Paris, he said, and had no idea that the weekly magazine belonged to the *Propaganda Staffel.* He then described his activities in the Resistance and his contacts with Allen Dulles in Geneva. "For my actions during World War II, I was awarded the *Rosette de la Résistance* and the *Croix de Guerre 1939–1945 avec palmes* [the War Cross with honors]."

Bettencourt described in detail his political career as a local representative, a member of Parliament, and a minister in several cabinets.

> In the course of my ministerial functions, I have been received by Mrs. Golda Meir and Foreign Minister Abba Eban. In 1973 I served as the representative of

France at the funeral of Israeli President Ben-Gurion.

I believe my public service and other activities during and since World War II indicate the falsity of any accusation that I collaborated with the Nazis or participated in the genocide that they wrought. I further believe that the renewed attention to my articles in *La Terre Française* half a century ago are attributable at least partly to persons who have distorted the facts to serve ulterior business motives. For example, your letter quotes a passage supposedly taken from an article in the December 1941 Christmas edition of the newspaper. Your quotation begins, 'The Jews of today . . . will be and already are vomited.' No such sentence appears in this article, which essentially retells the Christmas story.

Bettencourt was right. This sentence didn't appear in the Christmas edition of the newspaper.

It appeared in the Easter edition.

For a long time the red book wasn't revealed to the media. The Frydman brothers hoped that some of the Jewish organizations would publicly stand up and ask Bettencourt for explanations, as Congressman Engel did. After all, the anti-Semitic writings of André Bettencourt didn't concern only the Frydman brothers. This was a subject on which Jewish people should react. If nobody else took action by January 1995, the Frydman brothers decided, they would release the red book to the press.

This they did in February 1995. The revelations about Bettencourt exploded on the front pages of the Paris newspapers.

"L'Oréal embarrassed by the Vichy past of Mr. Bettencourt," said *Le Monde*'s headline. Inside, an entire page was devoted to the Bettencourt affair. "Until now," wrote Edwy Plenel, "the essays of Mr. Bettencourt in *La Terre Française* were only briefly mentioned in the right-wing press, and only one quotation was published in a recent book (*La Main droite de Dieu*, Seuil, 1994). It turns out that the essays were much more numerous than we thought, and their contents express a strong involvement branded by the National-Socialist seduction."

"Bettencourt caught up by his past," announced the *Parisien*.

Le Figaro carried Bettencourt's first reaction: "I am not anti-Semitic! . . . I wrote about twenty lines about the Jews that I sincerely regret." In another interview Bettencourt said: "I made a mistake by writing these articles in *La Terre Française*. I'll never regret it enough, and I apologize again today to the Jewish community. But nobody can question my past as a resistant since 1942 in François Mitterrand's MNPGD." He told *Le Parisien* that he was a victim of "a hateful plot."

Most articles carried official photographs of Bettencourt—a smiling, distinguished gentleman dressed in the dashing embroidered uniform of a member of the Académie. But a television reporter who came to interview Bettencourt found "a bitter, broken man."

Several journalists later spoke of pressures on their newspapers brought to bear by people close to L'Oréal. Edwy Plenel, *Le Monde*'s executive editor, said that after his articles on Bettencourt in March 1995, L'Oréal canceled an ad campaign in *Le Monde*. Plenel, after consulting with his editor in chief, Jean-Marie Colombani, called one of L'Oréal's lawyers and said to him, "Listen, you know me, we have covered many affairs in our paper, and if you [L'Oréal] adopt this kind of attitude, we are going to attack you publicly."

The lawyer immediately called Owen-Jones, and they found out that the orders to cancel the advertising had come from an overzealous employee in the publicity department. These orders were countermanded, and L'Oréal's ads returned to the prestigious pages of *Le Monde*.

The scandal soon made headlines in England, Switzerland, and other European countries. In the United States it received wide coverage. Serge Klarsfeld flew to New York and presented the incriminating articles in a press conference. He officially asked the U.S. immigration authorities to put Bettencourt's name on the watch list.

His request was vigorously supported by Congressmen Eliot Engel and Charles Schumer. On the Republican side, New York's junior senator Alfonse M. D'Amato and Governor George Pataki also backed Klarsfeld's request. On April 20, 1995, twenty U.S. congressmen, led by Engel, wrote a letter to Janet Reno, the U.S. attorney general, in support of Klarsfeld's initiative.

On May 16, 1995, an acting assistant attorney general, Kent Marcus, replied in a letter to Congressman Engel:

"The Criminal Division's Office of Special Investigations (OSI) has commenced an inquiry intended to ascertain whether Mr. Bettencourt, a citizen and resident of France, is eligible to enter the United States. . . . This inquiry will be concluded in a timely manner."

Marcus's letter to Engel, however, came long after the denouement of this tenebrous affair had taken place.

L'Oréal's president, Lindsay Owen-Jones, and his associates knew already in the fall of 1994 that very soon Bettencourt's past would be exposed in the press. In its new policy in Israel, L'Oréal had promised to contribute a million dollars to a campaign against traffic accidents, initiated by Knesset member Avraham Burg. On September 24, Jean Frydman met Burg and warned him that soon Bettencourt's past would be publicized, and Burg's association with L'Oréal might become awkward.

In late November 1994, the red book published by the Frydmans ended up in the hands of some top officials at L'Oréal. In early December several urgent meetings took place at the Centre Eugène Schueller. The atmosphere was gloomy. L'Oréal was just surfacing, exhausted and battered, from the boycott affair. It was just mending its fences with Israel and the Jewish community. It still had a trial upcoming: the Frydmans' suit against Cosmair in the United States. The American Jewish community was restive, U.S. congressmen were harshly attacking L'Oréal, and the calls for a boycott of L'Oréal products were multiplying.

The company couldn't afford another scandal. It would be exposed to the press onslaught against André Bettencourt as soon as the charges against him became known. Bettencourt might be Mr. L'Oréal, the owner of the company, but he had to go.

A top official of L'Oréal was charged with the task of talking to Bettencourt. According to certain sources, it was Owen-Jones himself. Some say that Jean-Pierre Meyers, Bettencourt's son-in-law, was also present but didn't intervene. Bettencourt was told, gently but firmly, that the forthcoming revelations about his past would embarrass L'Oréal and that he should step down.

It was a quiet coup d'état.

A L'Oréal board meeting was called for December 13, 1994. Shortly after, a spokesman for L'Oréal announced to the press that Senator André Bettencourt, "who represented the founding and controlling family on the board of L'Oréal, has stepped down as a director."

In addition to resigning from the vice presidency of L'Oréal, Bettencourt also announced that he would not run for senator again. The official reason for his resignation was his age. "I'll be seventy-six in April," he said, "and I want a peaceful life."

With the resignation of André Bettencourt from L'Oréal's board of directors, another drama came to an end: the ugly story of the parallel L'Oréal that had been a refuge for Nazi and Vichy collaborators for fifty years.

When André Bettencourt stepped down, he handed over the vice presidency of L'Oréal to his son-in-law, Jean-Pierre Meyers. This was poetic justice at its best. Not only was Meyers Jewish, but his family history also had powerful World War II resonance.

His grandfather, Rabbi Robert Meyers, had been the rabbi of Thionville in the Moselle, and later of Neuilly-sur-Seine. During the war he moved to Annecy, which was subsequently occupied by the Germans. In the summer of 1942 he was secretly contacted by a representative of General Charles de Gaulle, who wanted him to escape to London and become the Jewish chaplain for the Free French forces. He declined, believing that he shouldn't abandon his people in their hour of mortal danger, when they were threatened by the Vichy police and the Gestapo.

On November 15, 1942, while the German army was in the process of occupying the Free Zone, the prefect of the Haute-Savoie *département* offered to help the rabbi cross the border to Switzerland. Rabbi Meyers refused again, convinced that his place was in France, with his people. He agreed only that his children be sent to safety in Switzerland. He and his wife remained in Annecy, fully aware of the risk they were running.

Rabbi Robert Meyers and his wife were deported to Auschwitz.

They both died there.

Their son was employed at L'Oréal.

Their grandson took over the seat that had belonged to Eugène Schueller and André Bettencourt.

There are still trials and confrontations pending, in France and in America, in which Jean and David Frydman will oppose L'Oréal. The trial of Frydman against Cosmair, to be held in the United States, has not even been scheduled yet.

A foretaste of this trial was provided by the fining of L'Oréal by the U.S. Department of Commerce on August 29, 1995, after it was established that L'Oréal affiliate Parbel had violated the American antiboycott law. Parbel Florida, the successor to Helena Rubinstein, had broken the law by sending to L'Oréal headquarters in Paris several documents concerning its business with Israel. This had taken place in 1989, when L'Oréal was striving to convince the Boycott Bureau in Damascus of its compliance with the Arab strictures.

Following the heavy fine, Lindsay Owen-Jones wrote a letter to Abraham Foxman, the U.S. national director of the Anti-Defamation League. "I believe an international company like L'Oréal should have refused to place itself in such an unacceptable position and should not have replied to the boycott inquiries. . . . I am sorry that such correspondence was ever sent." Owen-Jones assured Foxman that "such action will not happen again."

Epilogue

One night in October 1995 Jean Frydman watched a television news broadcast in his Savyon home. The main item was a Jewish right-wing rally in Jerusalem, protesting Itzhak Rabin's peace initiative. The camera focused on some young activists who carried signs saying: "Rabin traitor" and "Rabin murderer." Some of them displayed posters representing Rabin in SS uniform.

Frydman was sickened. The supporters of the peace process, he thought, couldn't let this wave of hatred sweep Israel's streets and squares. They had to stand up and be counted. He called several of his friends and persuaded them to organize a huge rally in support of peace. He then met with Itzhak Rabin and Shimon Peres, and described his idea. The prime minister and the minister of foreign affairs reluctantly agreed. They were not convinced that Israel's silent majority would come to the rally, but decided to go along.

Jean Frydman and the former mayor of Tel Aviv, who organized the peace rally, had no doubt it would be a success. The rally was scheduled for Saturday, November 4, 1995. That night a huge crowd filled the Kings of Israel Square in Tel Aviv. Young people from all over the country, Jews and Arabs, displayed signs and slogans supporting the peace process, sang along with the famous singers performing on the podium, and cheered Rabin and Peres when they spoke of their dream of a peaceful Middle East. The rally was a tremendous success. Frydman and ex-mayor Lahat were on the podium, and were warmly thanked by several of the speakers for their initiative.

As the rally ended, Rabin and Peres went down the steps leading from the podium to the parking lot. Rabin suddenly turned back and returned to the podium. He hugged Jean Frydman. "Thank you, Jean," the prime minister said, "for giving me the two happiest hours of my life."

Less than a minute later he was shot in the back by a right-wing assassin.

In deep sorrow Frydman followed the prime minister's car to Tel Aviv's Ichilov Hospital, where he was told that Rabin had died.

Frydman didn't know how he would face Leah Rabin, the prime minister's widow. After all, the rally at which her husband died had been his idea. But when Leah Rabin saw him, she embraced him and said, "Jean, thanks to you Itzhak died a happy man."

WHERE THEY ARE TODAY

- President François Mitterrand ended his second term in office on May 17, 1995, and died of prostate cancer on January 8, 1996.
- L'Oréal flourished, enjoying several consecutive years of steadily increasing sales that were not affected by the 1989–1995 scandals.
- André Bettencourt resigned from the boards of directors of L'Oréal and Nestlé. He didn't run again for the French Senate. He is still president of Gesparal. He is still the subject of an inquiry by the U.S. Criminal Division's Office of Special Investigations.
- Lindsay Owen-Jones, unanimously praised as one of the best presidents L'Oréal ever had, led the company to record-breaking profits.
- François Dalle left his last official positions at L'Oréal and Paravision. On December 13, 1990, the strategic committee of L'Oréal—the main decision-making body of the company—was dissolved. François Dalle later moved to Switzerland.
- Marc Ladreit de Lacharrière left L'Oréal and is now the president of a financial company, Fimalac.
- Gérard Sanchez left L'Oréal.

• Pierre Castres Saint-Martin is vice president and financial director of L'Oréal.

• Michel Pietrini left the presidency of Paravision for the presidency of Lanvin perfumes in 1991, but had to resign after Lanvin failed to solve its financial difficulties.

• Catherine Morisse left Ariès and became vice president of the movie production company Légende, which produced among others the film *1492*.

• Claude de Kemoularia is still active at the Paribas bank.

• Raphael Berdugo became president of Paravision, sold its library of American movies, and decided to concentrate on French films.

• Jean-Pierre Getti was appointed judge at the International Court for Crimes against Humanity in The Hague, Holland.

• Jean-Louis Recordon was promoted to full colonel and transferred to the ministry of the interior, rue des Saussaies, in Paris.

• Jacques Mayoux still is the honorary president of the Société Générale bank.

• Charles Salzmann retired, and has no official activity.

• David Frydman continues to manage Ariès.

• Jean Frydman has been very active in promoting the peace process in the Middle East and conceived a plan for the solution of Gaza's economic problems.

SOURCES AND
ACKNOWLEDGMENTS

In 1994 I decided to write a book on *l'Affaire L'Oréal*. I first carried out an extensive study of the European, the American, and the Israeli daily and periodical press from 1989 until today. I then obtained and examined a large number of documents, letters, minutes, and notes concerning the murky relationship of L'Oréal and the Boycott Bureau, as well as the connected correspondence.

The thirty-eight full testimonies of the main protagonists of the affair, which were given under oath to Judge Getti, Colonel Recordon, and their aides, were of great use to me. So were the full texts of the legal proceedings in France (like the trials concerning the Mayoux report, one of which I attended on May 12, 1995), the complaints and arguments presented to the American courts, letters and petitions written by members of Congress in Washington, and correspondence between other American elected representatives and French personalities.

Several of the people I interviewed also gave me important documents from their private archives, and I'd like to thank Serge Klarsfeld in particular for the Corrèze files.

I read a great number of books on contemporary French history, mostly on the Second World War, on

François Mitterrand, on the Resistance, on the collaboration, and on La Cagoule. Several books were most useful for my particular purpose—Pierre Péan, *Une Jeunesse française*; Franz-Olivier Giesbert, *François Mitterrand*; Faux, Legrand, and Perez, *La Main droite de Dieu*; Pascale Froment, *René Bousquet*; Jacques Attali, *Verbatim*; Jean-François Chaigneau, *Le Dernier Wagon*; and Christian Bernadac, *Dagore, les carnets secrets de La Cagoule*.

I obtained more documents at several centers: the Centre de Documentation Juive Contemporaine, the National Archives, the Archives of the city of Paris, and the Press section at the Centre Beaubourg, all of them in Paris. While researching another subject, I found the files concerning the investigations against Eugène Schueller at the National Archives and the Archives of the City of Paris. I consulted Allen Dulles's private papers at the Mudd Library, in Princeton, and the OSS papers at the National Archives in Washington.

With all this material I was able to prepare a detailed chronology of the affair, and I could move to the next stage: the interviews. I interviewed about fifty people, some of them several times. I was asked not to mention the names of several people I interviewed, and several others asked not to be directly quoted; I respected their wishes. A partial list of those interviewed is found below.

The interviews, while most valuable, were rarely used as references or sources of information for the controversial questions that I treated. The narration of the boycott negotiations and the sorry past of some of L'Oréal's former leaders is exclusively based on abundant documentary evidence.

It is a pleasant duty for me to thank first and foremost Olivier Stupp, who showed tremendous devotion and zeal assisting me and bearing with me, which definitely is not an easy task. I am grateful too to Anne Salgue for her help in the early stages of my work.

I also thank all those, named or unnamed below, who agreed to give me their time to answer my questions.

Efraim Apter, Jacques Attali, Jean-Paul Azéma, Bruna Basini, Marc Boudier, Pierre-Marie Dioudonnat, David Frydman, Jean Frydman, Jean-Pierre Getti, Me William Goldnadel, Charles Gonnard, Peter Grose (by phone from New York), Jean-Edern Hallier, Avital Inbar, Me Michel Jobert, Me Bernard Jouanneau, Maurice Kahan, Jean Kahn, Me Georges Kiejman, Serge Klarsfeld, Me Théo Klein, Jean Lévy, Annette Lévy-Willard, Olivier Louis (by phone from London), Françoise-Marie Morel, Edwy Plenel, Jean-Marie Pontaut, Gad Propper, Colonel Ravanel, Colonel Jean-Louis Recordon, Jean-François Riva-Roveda (by phone from Peru), David Ruzie (by phone), Charles Salzmann, Me Didier Scornicki, Maurice Szafran, Hubert Vedrine, and others.

INDEX

· A NOTE ON THE TYPE ·

The typeface used in this book is a version of Times Roman, originally designed by Stanley Morison (1889–1967), the scholar who supervised Monotype's revivals of classic typefaces (Bembo) and commissioned new ones from Eric Gill (Perpetua), among others. Having censured *The Times* of London in an article, Morison was challenged to better it. Taking Plantin as a basis, he sought to produce a typeface that would be classical but not dull, compact without looking cramped, and would keep high readability on a range of papers. "*The Times* New Roman" debuted on October 3, 1932, and was almost instantly in great demand; it has become perhaps the most widely used of all typefaces (though the paper changed typeface again in 1972). Given its success, it is noteworthy that it was Morison's only original design. Ironically, he had pangs of conscience, writing later, "[William] Morris would have denounced [it]."